Insights from Common European Framework

edited by
KEITH MORROW

OXFORD
UNIVERSITY PRESS

UNIVERSITY PRESS

Great Clarendon Street, Oxford OX2 6DP

Oxford University Press is a department of the University of Oxford.
It furthers the University's objective of excellence in research, scholarship,
and education by publishing worldwide in

Oxford   New York

Auckland Bangkok Buenos Aires Cape Town Chennai
Dar es Salaam Delhi Hong Kong Istanbul Karachi Kolkata
Kuala Lumpur Madrid Melbourne Mexico City Mumbai
Nairobi São Paulo Shanghai Taipei Tokyo Toronto

ISBN 0 19 4309509

Typeset by MFK Mendip, Frome, Somerset
Printed in Spain

Contents

Acknowledgements

pp. 134–5, 136–7, 138–9, 140–1 from *A Common European Framework of Reference for Languages*

© Council of Europe.

pp. 132–3, 142–3 Tables 1a and 6 taken from Council of Europe 2003: 'Relating Language Examinations to the Common European Framework of Reference for Languages: Learning, Teaching, Assessment (CEF). Preliminary Pilot Version of a Proposed Manual' DGIV/EDU/LANG (2003) 5, Strasbourg

© Council of Europe 2003.

Introduction

This book reflects closely in style and content the work published in *ELT Journal*. Although free standing, it is in a sense a special issue of the *Journal*, with a series of articles focusing on a common theme.

The aims of this book are the same as the aims of the *Journal*, set out in each issue:

> *ELT Journal* is a quarterly publication for all those involved in the field of teaching English as a second or foreign language. It seeks to bridge the gap between the everyday practical concerns of ELT professionals and related disciplines such as education, linguistics, psychology, and sociology that may offer significant insights.

The title of this book indicates clearly that its focus is on 'insights'; and the gap it seeks to bridge is between 'the theory' as represented by the Common European Framework and 'the practice' when language-teaching professionals attempt to understand this theory and apply it in their work.

Each issue of the *Journal* contains articles reporting work of a similar nature. Ideas from the professional literature are applied in specific contexts, and are refined and developed as a result, leading the writer, and the reader, to a greater understanding of the original idea and of the ways it can influence—and be influenced by—practice.

This is exactly the aim of this collection. The Common European Framework is not fixed in stone; in some senses, it is still work in progress, as noted by Brian North at the end of his chapter in this book. Our aim is to:
- explain some of the background to the Framework
- clarify some of its contents
- explore some of its possible implications
- provide concrete examples of ways in which it has been used.

In this way we want to encourage more practitioners to engage in a principled way with the Framework, so that they are able to contribute to its further development.

This is important because the Framework is potentially very significant for language teaching—not just ELT—and is much talked about at the moment but little understood. One reason for this is because the only available documentation, published in the United Kingdom by Cambridge University Press, but also available to download on the web, is very difficult to follow. It is 250 pages of dense text interspersed with a myriad of charts and tables, whose relationship to each other is often hard to perceive.

None the less, aspects of the Framework are already having a major impact in:

- learning to learn—particularly through the European Language Portfolios
- teacher education—the Framework provides both an 'object' for study, and a source of ideas
- syllabus and course design—national education systems, e.g. in Italy, and publishers are increasingly taking account of the Framework in defining syllabuses and courses
- testing—an increasing number of examinations are being described in terms of the levels and the descriptors set out in the Framework.

These are the areas we have focused on in the chapters which make up this book. We hope you find what we have written interesting, challenging, and stimulating.

I would like to thank all the contributors for taking up the challenge to meet the impossible deadlines required by this project, and the team at Oxford University Press for performing a whole series of minor—and major—miracles to get the book out so quickly. My particular thanks go to Neus Figueras and Hanna Komorowska for their help in reviewing the contributions.

Keith Morrow
Editor, *ELT Journal*

References

Council of Europe. 2001. *Common European Framework of Reference for Languages: Learning, teaching, assessment.* Cambridge: Cambridge University Press.

Also available for download from http://www.coe.int/T/E/Cultural_Co-operation/education/Languages/Language_Policy/Common_Framework_of_Reference/1cadre.asp#TopOfPage

ELT Journal. See http://eltj.oupjournals.org.

Background to the CEF

Keith Morrow

Overview

This chapter puts the CEF in its context as a product of developments in language teaching sponsored by the Council of Europe over a period of more than 40 years. It outlines some of the basic features of the CEF, and attempts to clarify the purposes for which it is intended to be used.

The Council of Europe

The role of the Council of Europe in the development of ideas about language teaching is one of the best-kept secrets of the last 40 years. In a sense this reflects widespread ignorance among the population at large (certainly in the UK) about the Council of Europe itself. What is this organization? Why is it interested in language teaching? Is there a 'European agenda'?

In the context of this book, these are interesting questions, because the 'Common European Framework of Reference for Languages: Learning, Teaching, Assessment' —Common European Framework, or CEF for short (and throughout this book) is a product of the aims and aspirations of the Council of Europe, and is the development of work in this area that began in the late 1950s.

Why 'European'?

So the first point to clear up is that 'European' in the title has a specific meaning. It does not refer to a set of ideas that have a unique application in the continent of Europe and mean nothing elsewhere; it is not a product of the 'European Union', driven by nation states who have decided to find ways of working together within a common political and economic framework.

The Council of Europe has no connection with the European Union. While its work is 'political' in the broadest sense—aiming to safeguard human rights, democracy, and the rule of law in member countries—an important part of what it does is essentially cultural in nature rather than narrowly political or economic. A little bit of history may help to set the scene for what the CEF is about.

What is the Council of Europe?

Information about the Council of Europe is available on their web site www.coe.int. It is the continent' s oldest political organization, founded in 1949. It now groups together 45 countries, including 21 countries from Central and Eastern Europe. It is based in Strasbourg, and run by the Committee of Ministers, on which all member states are represented. The Council was set up to:

■ defend human rights, parliamentary democracy, and the rule of law

- develop continent-wide agreements to standardize member countries' social and legal practices
- promote awareness of a European identity based on shared values and cutting across different cultures.

In the context of this book, it is the last of these which is of greatest interest, since understanding the culture and recognizing the values of another country are only possible through language.

The Council of Europe and language teaching

One of the most striking features of 'Europe' viewed from the overall perspective of the Council of Europe is the range of mother tongues which its inhabitants use. It is not unique among the continents in this, of course. Africa and Asia also have a plethora of languages, but within North America the importance of a single mother tongue for official communication (apart from the use of French in Quebec) was arguably an important feature in the cultural unification of the constituent States of the USA and Provinces of Canada. In the USA the situation is becoming more complex now with the growth of pressure to recognize the need for bilingual policies, but historically the dominant role of English is undeniable. Similarly in Central and South America, the effect of the historical imposition of Spanish on large sections of the continent has been to create a means of sharing culture and experience among and between the citizens of the separate countries.

The European Babel

In Europe, however, the situation is very different. Each nation state, by and large, has its own language; some share a language with their neighbours, but others have two, three, or more languages which are used for official purposes. For the Council of Europe, the linguistic diversity of the continent therefore presented a challenge from the very start. If one of their aims was to encourage Europeans to look over the parapet of their own culture and see what was happening elsewhere in Europe, then an obvious barrier was a simple inability to understand linguistically what was going on.

One approach to this would have been to promote the use of a 'lingua franca' throughout Europe. English, French, German, or Spanish were on hand as internationally used and taught languages, or Esperanto or some similar invented language could have been promoted. However, this route was not followed for obvious reasons. The political sensibilities of the nations whose national language was not chosen ruled out the adoption of a 'natural' language; the selection of an artificial language would have placed a huge barrier in the way of international cultural communication.

In addition, it was realized early on that the languages of Europe constitute an essential part of the European cultural heritage. An organization interested in promoting access to culture needed to safeguard these languages and encourage their use, not sideline them.

For these reasons, then, the Council of Europe has long seen the promotion of language teaching/learning as one of its major priority areas, with the development of inter-cultural awareness viewed as an essential part of the development of competence in another language or other languages.

Plurilingualism

In the CEF the term 'plurilingualism' is introduced to describe the focus of the work of the Council of Europe in this area. For a full explanation of this term, see CEF 2001: 4, but briefly it implies action on the part of governments and individuals. Governments have the responsibility to extend the range of language learning opportunities, and exposure to other languages available to their citizens; individuals should be helped through language teaching, and the development of their own learning skills, to extend their ability to communicate, however laboriously and incompletely, with users of another language. To do this they should be helped to draw on their own competence in that language, however limited, and on the range of skills and awarenesses they bring from using their own language and other languages they may have learnt. Plurilingualism therefore recognizes that many people have some degree of competence in another language. The job of language teaching is to make them aware of this, and to nurture and encourage this competence.

The Council of Europe and developing approaches to language teaching

One of the first concrete steps taken by the Council of Europe in this area was their support for the development in the late 1950s of 'Le français fondamental', a specification of a basic grammar and vocabulary for French, and 'Voix et images de France', an audiovisual course for adults learning French.

This focus on teaching languages to adults was characteristic of much of the early work of the Council. In fact, what was arguably its most significant achievement before the production of the CEF, took place specifically under the auspices of its 'Committee for Out of School Education'. This was the work in the 1970s which led to the development of notional-functional syllabuses, the Threshold Level, and the birth of the communicative approach. While the ideas behind these have been taken up and refined outside the context of their original development, it is important to realize that it was the Council of Europe that set this context, and provided the framework within which this development could take place.

The motivation for this work lay in the development of a 'unit-credit' system which would enable learners to study 'units' of work (in specific notional functional areas) and gain 'credit' for these.

This was a complete break with earlier approaches to language teaching/learning, where the learner was engaged in a seemingly never-ending struggle to learn ever more complex aspects of the language. Here areas of study were presented which had an immediate 'surrender value'; the language learnt was of immediate practical application in the world outside the classroom. With its emphasis on using language for purposes of practical communication, and its specification of objectives which could be reached with only a partial mastery of the language, this was a direct forerunner of ideas developed in a more complete form in the CEF, and its impact on language teaching throughout the world is hard to exaggerate.

Through the 1980s the Council of Europe was involved in a number of initiatives to build on the ideas incorporated in the Threshold Level. The Waystage was developed as a lower-level set of objectives, a multimedia TV-based course *Follow Me* was produced based on this, and a large programme of teacher training workshops was organized.

In the late 1980s and into the 1990s, the changed political situation in Central and Eastern Europe lent fresh impetus to the work of the Council of Europe in the area of language learning, as a number of new member states became involved in its activities. From 1989–97 a major project was undertaken called 'Language learning for European citizenship', providing guidelines for the reform and development of language teaching in these new member states.

The concern of the Council of Europe with using education in its broadest sense, including language education, to promote human values is captured in this caption taken from its Education home page:

> helping to incorporate the principles of human rights, democracy, tolerance and mutual respect, the rule of law and peaceful resolution of conflicts into the daily practice of teaching and learning.

The Common European Framework

The formal origins of the CEF date back to 1991, when it was agreed that

> the mutual recognition of qualifications, and communication concerning objectives and achievement standards would be greatly facilitated if they were calibrated according to agreed common reference standards, purely descriptive in nature.
> (Trim: 2001: 5)

The aim was to provide a means of developing language teaching in Europe by finding a way to compare the objectives and achievement standards of learners in different national (and local) contexts. But almost inevitably the work carried out to meet this aim has resulted in a document with a far wider application, because it has meant an examination and codification of what Trim (2001: 5) calls:

> language use and the many 'competences' i.e. the shared knowledge and skills which enable users of a language to communicate with each other. Wherever possible, these are separately calibrated with brief descriptors defining six levels of proficiency.

This is a monumental undertaking, and the result—over 250 pages in the English version—is both weighty and comprehensive.

Comprehensiveness and complexity

It is precisely this characteristic that is one of the strengths and paradoxically one of the weaknesses of the CEF in its present form. In documenting the many competences which language users deploy in communication, and in defining different levels of performance in these competences, the authors of the Framework have made explicit the true complexity of the task that confronts learners—and teachers—of a language.

The reaction of many readers who approach the Framework looking for guidance in their work, as course or test designers, materials writers,

Keith Morrow

teacher educators, or classroom teachers, is to find the sheer amount of detail, the range of descriptors, and the plethora of terminology completely baffling. And it has to be said that the published versions of the CEF are not exactly user-friendly. There is little to guide the first-time reader around the material; the print is small, the layout dense and 'heavy', the language itself is ponderous and often convoluted; specialist terminology abounds, and is often used in ways which seem idiosyncratic—and there are seemingly endless tables and descriptors whose relationship to one another is very difficult to discern.

And yet, like good literature, the CEF repays, and deserves, careful study. No-one expects the blueprint for the design of an aircraft to be 'easy' bedtime reading, so why should we expect the blueprint for the use of what is arguably the most complex of our human learnt (or acquired) behaviours to be simple? Of course, there is scope for improvement in presentation, and perhaps most obviously, different users need to be given easier 'ways-in' to specific parts of the book of relevance to their own interests and needs. But it is the richness and range of the material that is so impressive, and of so much potential benefit to its users.

We may want to simplify aspects of it for particular purposes—indeed the Framework specifically invites users to pick and choose the bits of it they want to make use of—but in the same way that passengers, pilots, and airline company directors want to know that their planes are engineered to comprehensive specifications, so learners, teachers, and ministers of education want to know that decisions about language teaching are based on a full account of the competences that need to be developed. For the first time, such an account is now available.

What is the CEF for?

The full title of the CEF is 'The Common European Framework of Reference for Languages—Learning, Teaching, Assessment'. The key words in this are unfortunately two which are often left out: of reference. As noted above, the original aim of the project which led to the production of the CEF was to facilitate 'mutual recognition of qualifications, and communication concerning objectives and achievement standards'. The contents of the Framework are therefore designed principally to act as a frame of reference in terms of which different qualifications can be described, different language learning objectives can be identified, and the basis of different achievement standards can be set out.

Description not prescription

The most important characteristic of the CEF is implicit in this aim. It is a descriptive framework, not a set of suggestions, recommendations, or guidelines. This point is made explicitly in the Introduction to the Framework, and is picked up by several contributors to this book, but it bears repeating here.

Some see homogenization, standardization, or bureaucratic meddling behind initiatives which have a 'European' stamp. Whatever the justification—or otherwise —of these fears in other areas, the CEF is clean in this regard. As Frank Heyworth comments in the next chapter, this does not mean that the Framework is unprincipled, or totally neutral in its view of what language learning is, what the role of the learner is, or—above all—what the value of language learning is. But it does mean that the CEF is not dogmatic about objectives, about syllabus design, or about classroom methodology. In all these areas, and many others, it sets out the range of options, enabling a specific course or a specific examination to be described in terms that will identify similarities to, and differences from, other courses and examinations.

Raising awareness

This was the original aim, but the use and value of the CEF goes beyond this. Teachers, course designers, curriculum developers, and examination boards can engage with the CEF as a way of describing their current practice not in order to compare it in a neutral way with practice in other contexts, but in order to critique it in its own terms, and to improve it by drawing on ideas and resources set out in the Framework.

Earlier, the CEF was compared to a blueprint; in this sense, it is more like a detailed map. Everybody involved in language teaching/learning is involved in a journey of some kind. The CEF does not prescribe the route you should take, but it gives you details of the topography so you can plan your own—or so you can look again at the one you normally take to see if it is still the best. As noted above, one of the potential difficulties with the CEF is that the map is so detailed that you may not always be able to see the wood from the trees—but at least you should avoid getting stuck in a rut!

What is in the Common European Framework?
Common Reference Levels

At the heart of the CEF are the Common Reference Levels—the global scale (see Document I in the Reference documents section of this book). This is a broad description of what a user of a language can 'do' at six different levels of performance ranging from 'basic' (A1, A2) through 'independent' (B1, B2) to 'proficient' (C1, C2). They function as a reference point both for descriptions of levels/achievement, and for definitions of objectives. They give a peg on which to hang labels such as 'pre-intermediate', 'university level', or 'year 3', and they allow us to specify what do we want our learners to be able to do at a certain level.

Like any attempt to capture language performance in terms of language, the specifications, or 'descriptors' as they are called, cannot be absolutely precise. As an example, here is the first sentence from level B1:

> Can understand the main points of clear standard input on familiar matters regularly encountered in work, school, leisure, etc. Can deal with most situations likely to arise whilst travelling in an area where the language is spoken.

What are 'the main points'? Who decides? Is what is 'clear' in my opinion, 'clear' in yours? Are the situations likely to arise when I am travelling the same as the ones likely to arise when *you* are travelling? And how many is 'most'?

Problems such as these mean that these global descriptors can in themselves be no more than indicative. But there is evidence from the work of North and Schneider (1998) that they are meaningful, and that descriptors of performance in specific areas, e.g. reading or writing, or of

Keith Morrow

specific competences, e.g. identifying cues and inferring, or taking the floor (turntaking) can be reliably 'calibrated' against these level descriptions.

Sub-scales

In focusing on the 'global' scale of performance at six levels, it is important to realize that this is just the tip of the iceberg. Underpinning this global definition of performance are descriptions in terms of a large range of other competences which make up the abilities of a user of a language at a given level.

Common Reference Levels: global scale

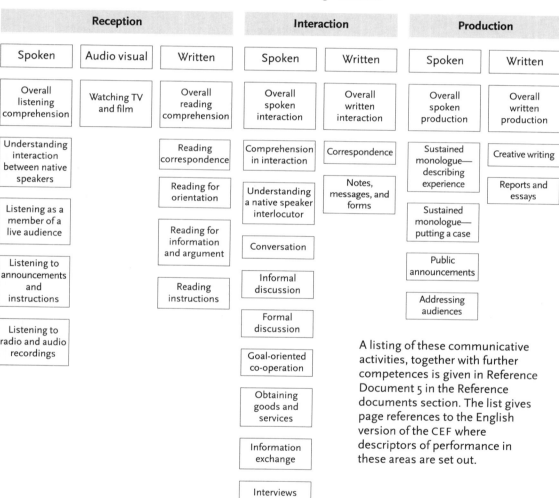

A listing of these communicative activities, together with further competences is given in Reference Document 5 in the Reference documents section. The list gives page references to the English version of the CEF where descriptors of performance in these areas are set out.

FIGURE 1 Communicative activities which underlie the global scale

Figure 1 shows the range of communicative activities which underlie the global scale. In all these areas, descriptors have been developed (usually at all six levels). This list of communicative activities is clearly not exhaustive. In 'written production', for example, it is easy to imagine

Background to the CEF

other types of writing which language users may need to produce. But by producing these 'illustrative' areas, and giving information about the methodology followed to produce the scales of performance within them, the CEF makes is possible for users to produce their own specifications for their own specific purposes.

As well as descriptions of communicative activities, the CEF sets out scales of performance in other competences, e.g. communication strategies, and language competence. A listing of these is provided in Document 5 in the Reference documents section of this book, giving page references to the English version of the CEF where the various scales are set out.

Of course, the CEF contains a lot more than the scales and descriptors discussed here, but these are the core. Other aspects of the content are discussed by Frank Heyworth in the next chapter, and by other authors as they focus on the practical application of the Framework in different contexts and for different purposes.

Does the CEF work?

Certainly the CEF is not without its critics. Issues of style and presentation have been raised in this chapter, and many would-be users share the negative reactions of some of Hanna Komorowska' s students (see p.57)

> Students criticized both the length of the document and its structure, pointing to overlaps, especially in chapters related to language use, language learning and language teaching; they also complained about never-ending typologies and lists.

Many find themselves in the position that Julia Keddle (see p.43) articulates:

> I find that I am both an enthusiast and a critic.

Some have gone even further. A recent publication edited by a group of German-speaking academics (Bausch, Christ, and Königs 2002) makes sweeping criticisms of the Framework. They argue that it is weak on theoretical grounds (lack of a consistent underlying theory, vague and inconsistent use of terminology) and suspect in terms of its practical use (focused on the commercial needs of publishers, and especially international testing agencies such as members of ALTE—the Association of Language Testers in Europe). Tellingly, for a document produced to facilitate intercultural awareness, the authors of the CEF are criticized by this German-speaking group for ignoring professional literature written in German, and drawing exclusively on sources in French and English.

So the jury is out. However, despite the reservations of some of her students, Hanna Komorowska considers the CEF to be worth the effort; Julia Keddle continues to work with the Framework despite her frustrations. The present book is about ' insights'—and the general message is that by working to gain insights into the CEF, we can gain very powerful insights into our work in the field of language teaching. Yet it would be astonishing if a work of the scope and the potential

Keith Morrow

importance of the CEF were not to be critiqued, and in the way of the world some of these criticisms will be fair and valid—others will not. As the anonymous reviewer of Bausch, Christ, and Königs' book says on the German Amazon web site:

> Es ist mein Eindruck, dass nicht alle den Referenzrahmen gut gelesen haben.
> *(I have the impression that not all (the contributors to this book) have read the CEF closely.)*

Anybody picking up the CEF can understand the temptation not to. But please let no one say that about the contributors to this volume.

References

Amazon http://www.amazon.de (Accessed December 2003)

Bausch, K-R., H. Christ, and **F. G. Königs** (eds.). 2002. *Der Gemeinsame europäische Referenzrahmen für Sprachen in der Diskussion.* Tübingen: Gunter Narr Verlag.

Council of Europe Education home page http://www.coe.int/T/E/Cultural_Co-operation/education/ (Accessed January 2004).

North, B. and **G. Schneider.** 1998. 'Scaling descriptors for language proficiency scales'. Language Testing 15/2: 217–62.

Trim, J. 2001. 'The Work of the Council of Europe in the field of Modern Languages, 1957–2001' (mimeo). Paper given at a Symposium to mark the European Day of Languages 26 September 2001 at the European Centre for Modern Languages, Graz.

The author

Keith Morrow is a teacher and teacher-trainer, with a special interest in language testing. He is the editor of *ELT Journal*.

Why the CEF is important

Frank Heyworth

Overview

Why should teachers struggle through the 250 densely written, rather opaque pages of the Common European Framework? It is true that it is not light reading, but the CEF provides a comprehensive account of an approach to language education which language teachers, teacher trainers, and academic managers need at least to consider, together with a set of resources which can have practical applications in the planning and delivery of language courses. The different aspects are all dealt with in detail in the later chapters of the book; in this chapter I will try to describe some of the background to each of them, and to explore why and how they are important.

Introduction

Here are some of the questions addressed in the Framework:

1 Why should we learn languages? Are they a simple tool for communication, or are there educational and social aims we need to take into account?

2 What do we mean by learning a language? What does communicative competence consist of, apart from knowing grammar and vocabulary?

3 What are levels? Is it feasible to create a standardized set of scales for describing what learners can do, which can apply to different languages, and which are relevant to different language users?

4 How do we decide on learning objectives? How do we help learners to set realistic, achievable goals?

5 How do teachers make reasoned choices among all the methodological options open to them?

6 What issues are involved in the assessment of learners?

I will look at each of these in turn.

Why should we learn languages?
The value of language learning

In the Council of Europe's work over more than 40 years, there has been a constant and developing affirmation that learning languages has educational value for personal development in addition to its practical value. The Common European Framework (CEF 2001: 4) states as one of its objectives:

> To promote methods of modern language teaching which will strengthen independence of thought, judgement and action, combined with social skills and responsibility.

Approaches which emphasize learner autonomy and co-operation are seen not just as effective teaching methods, but as having value in themselves. Implicitly, the Council of Europe is stating a political agenda for language teaching as an instrument in the development of 'Democratic Citizenship in Europe'—which was the title of the Council's modern languages project from 1997 to 2001.

Although the CEF denies that it is prescriptive:

> we do not set out to tell practitioners what to do, or how to do it
> (CEF 2001: Introduction)

it is far from neutral. Throughout the CEF there is a concentration on the language learner and user both as an individual and a social agent.

> [Language learning is important] in the interests of greater mobility, more effective international communication combined with respect for identity and cultural diversity, more intensive personal interaction, improved working relations and a deeper mutual understanding.
> (CEF 2001: 5)

The aims of language learning

Many language teachers will think this overstates the importance of language teaching, and will say that their job is simply to help learners to master the language, but the issue is an important one.

Communicative approaches to language teaching and learning offer opportunities to choose the topics to be addressed. Course books frequently reduce the content of language teaching to everyday banality and stereotyped situations and characters, whereas language teachers could choose to use the opportunity to provide useful information, stimulate reflection, address social issues, and promote values in ways which could contribute to both personal development and social awareness.

Among the aims stated or implied in the CEF are:
- The development of European citizenship, with an educated European understanding several languages, able to study and travel in many countries, knowledgeable about, and having respect for many different nationalities and national cultures.
- The conviction that knowing different languages is a powerful factor in intellectual development, encouraging open-mindedness and flexibility, contributing to the development of other skills.
- The commitment to life-long language learning, accepting that it is unlikely that schools can predict exactly which languages their students are going to need, and that therefore the aim should be to train them to become good language learners, capable of acquiring the particular languages as they meet the need for them.
- The idea that language study offers opportunities to acquire independence and autonomy as learners, that it can be learnt in ways which encourage co-operation and other social values.

This pre-supposes that language teaching has a privileged position—because there is a freedom, not available to maths or geography teachers, to be found in both the choice of content and in the methodological approach. When they are teaching learners to communicate in the foreign language, teachers can choose the topics to be discussed, and can therefore introduce issues of social and educational relevance; In terms of methodology, communicative approaches to teaching include co-operation in learning, and the development of reflective and autonomous learning habits.

Knowing a language needs more than just grammar and vocabulary. It involves knowing what language is appropriate for use in a given situation—sociolinguistic competence—and how appropriacy differs from one culture to another—(inter-cultural competence). The CEF suggests that in order to do this well, learners need to develop concepts of cultural differences, and attitudes of linguistic tolerance and respect.

Some potential problems

There are dangers in this approach: of trying to do amateur social engineering; of supposing language teachers not to be affected by intercultural prejudice; perhaps of assuming that knowing someone else's language automatically promotes understanding and respect. What, specifically, are language teachers expected to do to achieve this? There will need to be much more usable descriptions of cultural differences and intercultural competences, in order to achieve teachability linked to successful language learning.

The purpose of the CEF, embodied in the common reference levels, and the emphasis on a broad range of competences, is to provide resources to make this approach to language education feasible.

What do we mean by learning a language?
An action-based approach

The emphasis throughout the CEF is on how languages are used and what learners/users can do with the language—on language being action-based, not knowledge-based. The introduction to the Framework summarizes a major aspect of its contents, as follows:

> Language learning activities are based on the needs, motivations, and characteristics of learners:
>
> What will they need to do with the language?
> What will they need to learn in order to do what they want?
> What makes them want to learn?
> What sort of people are they?
> What knowledge, skill, and experiences do their teachers possess?
> What access do they have to resources?
> How much time can they afford to spend?
> (CEF 2001: 4)

The CEF deals with all these aspects, and in this way it provides a reasoned and detailed description of what the 'Communicative Approach' implies: needs analysis based on the learners' functional objectives; the involvement of the learner and learner motivation as a central feature; the idea of a co-operative relationship between learner and teacher; and a realistic way of fitting the course to the resources available, not to an abstract goal of perfection.

Frank Heyworth

This view of language learning makes it clear that it is not just a question of linguistic competence, of learning grammar, vocabulary, and pronunciation.

Competences

The CEF describes language use and learning as competence-based, and treats competences from a global, plurilingual, and pluricultural point of view:

> A given individual does not have a collection of distinct and separate competences to communicate depending on the languages he/she knows, but rather a plurilingual and pluricultural competence encompassing the full range of the languages available to him/her.
> (CEF 2001: 168)

However, all this individual competence is partial:

> All knowledge of language is partial, however much of a 'mother tongue' or 'native language' it seems to be. It is always incomplete, never as developed or perfect in an ordinary individual as it would be for the utopian 'ideal native speaker'.
> (CEF 2001: 169)

The CEF claims that the learning of partial competences for a specific purpose is not limited to that purpose, since other knowledge and skills are acquired at the same time which enable the learner to do other things. It also maintains that:

> Those who have learnt one language also know a great deal about many other languages without necessarily realizing that they do. The learning of further languages generally facilitates the activation of this knowledge and increases awareness of it, which is a factor to be taken into account rather than proceeding as if it did not exist.
> (CEF 2001: 70)

These two notions are important ones for language teachers to be aware of:

1 The idea of a 'unique individual competence' including the whole repertoire of languages and competences available provides a justification for more emphasis to be placed on developing strategies and skills for 'learning to learn languages' since the learner can apply these skills to learning or acquiring other languages. It encourages learners and teachers to be more aware of the usefulness of considering how the specific language being taught/learnt relates to the rest of the learner's overall linguistic resources. Teachers sometimes assume that a beginner starts from scratch, but in fact most have experiences of other languages and skills and knowledge they can apply usefully to learning the new language.

2 The concept of partial competences reinforces the need for negotiation of objectives with learners, and recognition of the fact that not everyone has to set off on the journey to learn the whole of the language. Learning a language is not an 'all or nothing' undertaking. The various descriptor scales to be found throughout the CEF provide descriptions of partial competences and these can be used by teachers as a source for discussion

of objectives with learners—this includes identification both of what they would like to learn and what is not needed.

The CEF provides a useful reminder to language teachers to extend the range of their teaching beyond the narrowly linguistic by giving an insight into the range of different competences involved in learning a language. These include:

- pragmatic competences: the user/learner's knowledge of the principles according to which messages are:
  — organized, structured, and arranged ('discourse competence')
  — used to perform communicative functions ('functional competence')
  — sequenced according to the user's internal models of how communication takes place ('design competence').
- sociolinguistic competence: the knowledge and skills required to deal with the social dimension of language use
- intercultural competence: knowledge, awareness, and understanding of the relation between the learner's world, and the world of users of the target language
- strategic competence: being aware of the communicative process and being able to 'manage' it
- existential competence: the learner's personality features, motivations, attitudes, beliefs, etc.

What are levels? Can they be described and standardized?

At the core of the Common European Framework is the Common Scale of Reference (see Document 1 in the Reference documents section of this book; also Council of Europe 2001: 24ff). This is sometimes referred to as the global scale, to distinguish it from the other descriptor scales provided in specific areas.

This scale, and the others in the CEF, have a number of significant feature:

- All the statements in the scales are positive, and are intended to demonstrate that even 'low' levels of language learning have value and worth. The last sentence of A1 could have been expressed as 'cannot understand when people talk too fast', but instead it has been expressed positively by definition of the support which will allow communication—'provided the other person talks slowly and clearly and is prepared to help'.
- Traditionally, language use is described in terms of the four skills of listening, reading, writing, and speaking. The CEF global scales present a description based on 'reception', 'production', 'interaction', and 'mediation'. Mediation includes translation and interpretation, as well as other ways of using language to get meaning across, such as periphrasis, simplification, etc. The CEF description allows us to distinguish between spoken production and spoken interaction, and encourages us to look at the skills as being integrated rather than isolated.
- The global scale is also the basis of a self-assessment grid which uses the descriptors as 'can do' statements and expands them to describe performance in relation to five skills, related to three areas. These are Understanding (Listening and Reading), Speaking (Spoken interaction

Frank Heyworth

and Spoken production), and Writing. (See Document 2 in the Reference documents section of this book; also Council of Europe 2001: 26ff.)

- The level descriptors are intended to be independent of each other and are not, of course, related to specific languages. They are not designed to be split up into equal chunks of time in a syllabus, and it will take longer to move from B2 to C1 than from A1 to A2, for example.
- They are not intended to describe the language user's competence from beginner to native speaker. Level C2 includes descriptions of the high level, complex language an educated, highly trained learner of a foreign language may be able to use, and it includes skills which a majority of native speakers do not possess.
- The six level system does not mean that it is intended to divide the whole language learning world into six. Employers may only need the three broad levels; schools which need to show progress can sub-divide the levels, theoretically as many times as they wish, though it is likely that it will be very difficult to distinguish in words more than 10 or 12.

Uses of scales

Descriptor scales are not new, but those of the Common Scale are more rigorously designed than most; they form a foundation for the creation of 'can do' checklists, which—in the European Language Portfolio and elsewhere—are used as a basis for self-assessment. This scale has had so much influence on teaching in many countries that people often speak of it as if it was the whole of the Framework.

The levels are being used as the reference for setting objectives, for assessment and for certification in many contexts around Europe—in the Finnish, Italian, Hungarian, and French school systems; in all the 21 suites of language examinations of ALTE (the Association of Language Testers in Europe). Already coursebooks based, or claiming to be based on the levels, are being published. This offers many advantages—the words 'intermediate' and 'advanced' are vague terms which tend to be interpreted very differently in different contexts. The scale from A1 to C2 makes level statements more transparent, and the scale is increasingly being used to describe and compare levels both within and across languages.

All of this means that operational knowledge of the scales, and the ability to use them in course planning and in assessment, are useful skills for all language teachers. In many contexts they are already providing the 'common language for practitioners' which is one of the aims of the CEF.

Specialized scales

The global Common Reference Scale is complemented by additional more specialized scales. These descriptor scales—and there are 58 of them—are all based on the reference levels, and are valuable sources for curriculum and syllabus design. For a list of these scales and information about where to find them in the CEF, please see Document 5 in the Reference documents section of this book. They provide a set of operational instruments for more focused and targeted teaching of communication skills, and are divided into those describing:

1 communicative activities—with general skills scales complemented by specific uses—for example, interviewing and being interviewed, reading instructions

2 communication strategies—such as asking for clarification, and turntaking

3 communicative language competences—describing linguistic range and accuracy, sociolinguistic competence, and pragmatic competence, including flexibility, coherence, and spoken fluency.

Overall they provide a very useful source of level-related material for curriculum design and assessment. And teachers and course planners can use the six-point scale as a basis for the development of further specialized scales they may need.

How do we decide on learning objectives?

A transparent system of describing purpose, content, and levels is essential for setting objectives and standards and for measuring them. Chapter 3 of the CEF deals with the general question of 'Scaling' and 'Levels', and examines the issues related to describing learner proficiency. It describes the difficulties involved in producing level descriptors which clearly distinguish between different levels, which are comprehensible to the learners and other users, and which contribute positively to the learning process.

A distinction is made between user-oriented scales, which are designed for learners, employers, and other judges of level reached—they tell us what the learner can do—and assessor-oriented scales, which guide the evaluator in making reliable judgements about how well the learner performs. These are particularly important for examination boards since examinations are increasingly being identified by reference to the global levels, and the Council of Europe is preparing a manual with indications about the way the matching of their content to CEF levels should be approached. For more details of this, see the chapter by Brian North in this book.

The application of the descriptors is complemented by the comprehensive account of language use and the needs of the language learner. Of particular relevance to needs analysis is the diagram in CEF 2001: 48–9. This is reproduced as Document 3: 'External contexts of use' in the Reference documents section of this book. It provides categories for describing how learners use language and therefore how they can set learning objectives. The concepts of domain—personal, public, occupational, educational—and the descriptive categories of location, institution, person, object, event, operation, and text, provide a framework for the design of needs analysis questionnaires, and for the definition of outcomes.

Again the relevance for teachers is in the way the CEF broadens and makes systematic the description of what is involved in learning, teaching, and assessing.

Frank Heyworth

How do teachers make reasoned methodological choices?	CEF Chapter 6 deals with the processes of language learning and teaching. It provides a useful guide to teaching processes and the options open to teachers. It does not, however, give strong guidance on how the different options can be combined in a coherent process—the Framework does not seek to be prescriptive —but can be used as source of material for reflection and for teacher development activities.
Dealing with errors and mistakes	For example, there is a section dealing with the issue of errors and mistakes (CEF 2001: 155). It distinguishes the two terms—errors being examples of the learner's interlanguage, which demonstrate her/his present level of competence, whereas mistakes occur when learners, like native speakers sometimes, do not bring their knowledge and competence into their performance—i.e. they know the correct version, but produce something which is wrong.

This distinction is not new, but it provides a basis for considering in the next section, a list of possible attitudes to mistakes and errors. What do you think about them? Are errors and mistakes evidence of failure to learn? Or is it the case that 'errors are an inevitable, transient product of the learner's developing interlanguage'? And what do we do about them? There is a list of possible pedagogic approaches to error—among them 'all errors and mistakes should be immediately corrected by the teacher'; 'errors should be corrected only where they interfere with communication'; 'all errors should be noted and corrected when doing so does not interfere with communication'. The comprehensive list of options can provide a stimulus for teachers to consider the issue in a wider framework than their own experience, and like the other sections of this chapter, it ends with a set of reflection points:

> Users of the Framework may wish to consider, and where appropriate state their attitude to, an action in response to learner errors and mistakes, and whether the same or different criteria apply to:
> — phonetic errors and mistakes
> — orthographic errors and mistakes
> — vocabulary errors and mistakes
> — morphological errors and mistakes
> — syntactic errors and mistakes
> — sociolinguistic and sociocultural errors and mistakes
> — pragmatic errors and mistakes.
> (CEF 2001: 156)

Learning and acquisition

Another example of a distinction which the CEF reminds us of is that between 'learning' and 'acquisition'. The authors point out that the learning process involves both learning and acquiring competences and developing:

> [The] ability to put these competences into action in the production/reception of spoken utterances/written texts to express and understand meanings, to interpret and negotiate meaning in context and to engage in communicative activities.
> (CEF 2001: Introduction)

It outlines the various theories of how languages are learnt—including the debate as to whether it is a more or less innate human information-processing activity, requiring only exposure to language, or whether explicit teaching and study are needed, to accelerate the process. The place of conscious learning and structured practice is discussed.

Options and autonomy

The main feature of this section is the way in which it presents options to the teacher. The methodological ideas are not in themselves new, but the sheer range of possibilities which are identified is interesting and impressive.

An interesting implication of the presentation of options in this way is that it pre-supposes teachers who are responsible, autonomous individuals capable of making informed choices, and acting upon them. This is precisely the view of the language learner/user upon which the CEF is built, and it reminds us of the political vision which underlies the work of the Council of Europe.

What issues are involved in the assessment of learners?

Many have perceived the impact of the Common Scale of Reference as being mainly in the area of assessment and certification, especially in relation to the standardization and comparison of results. It will be a pity if this causes teachers to lose sight of the main message of the CEF as a whole, where the emphasis is on a learner-centred approach.

Self-assessment

Self-assessment is central to this. The self-assessment grid (see Document 2 in the Reference documents section of this book) with descriptors beginning 'I can …' can be used for learners to look at their own competences in relation to the scale. This has been adopted as a key feature of the European Language Portfolio, and the development of self-assessment checklists to accompany the grid have been used effectively as a way of stimulating learner motivation and involvement. A research project carried out by Guenther Schneider and Brian North for the Swiss National Research Council (Schneider and North 2000) also showed a high level of reliability for self-assessment, with high correlations to teacher assessment and examination results.

Issues in assessment

Chapter 9 deals with Assessment, and describes in detail the different options which need to be taken into account in the development of assessment activities. It distinguishes clearly between norm-referenced and criterion-referenced assessment, between achievement and proficiency testing, and between formative and summative assessment. It raises the problems of how to measure communicative as well as linguistic competence, and quotes examples of different approaches to these. In this way it is a good general introduction to assessment issues.

The common reference levels are key elements towards the achievement of a common vocabulary and a common set of standards for talking about language knowledge, skills, and achievement. As such, they are important factors in assuring quality and measuring it. The appendices include the ALTE scales, with 'can do' statements for tourism, work, and study, and the DIALANG scales for self-assessment. (See the chapter by Ari Huhta and Neus Figueras in this book.)

Frank Heyworth

The CEF provides an important set of resources for comprehensive coverage of the different components of competence in language knowledge and use. They can be used for assessment of present level and aims, for specifying the objectives and assessing the outcomes of a course. Taken together, Chapters 3 and 9 provide a comprehensive guide to achieving a meaningful, rigorous, and comprehensive assessment of language achievement and proficiency.

Conclusions

The rest of this book will look at various specific uses of the Common European Framework. I think its general importance for all those involved in language teaching is:

- as a stimulus to think about language teaching and learning in a broader, more coherent way
- as a set of resources for planning, implementing, and assessing learner-centred, action-based language learning and teaching
- as a political statement of the value of language learning for individual development, and for social cohesion and for tolerance.

References

Council of Europe. 2001. *Common European Framework of Reference for Languages: Learning, Teaching, Assessment.* Cambridge: Cambridge University Press.
Also available for download from http://www.coe.int/T/E/Cultural_Co-operation /education/Languages/Language_Policy/ Common_Framework_of_Reference/1cadre.asp# TopOfPage
Schneider, G. and **B. North.** 2000. *Fremdsprachen können—was heisst das? Skalen zur Beschreibung, Beurteilung und Selbsteinschätzung der fremdsprachlichen Kommunikationsfähigkeit.* Chur/Zürich: Verlag Rüeger.

The author

Frank Heyworth is Secretary General of EAQUALS (the European Association of Quality Language Services) and has played a prominent role in setting up and running the Association's inspection scheme. He was previously Director General of the Eurocentres Foundation, and has participated in numerous projects of the Council of Europe. He is co-author of the *User Guide on Quality Assurance* for the Common European Framework, and has produced studies on innovative approaches to the organization of language education and the concept of quality in language teaching for the European Centre for Modern Languages, Graz.

The European Language Portfolio

Peter Lenz

Overview

The European Language Portfolio (ELP) and the Common European Framework of Reference for Languages (CEF) were developed simultaneously between 1991 and 2001, and influenced each other in many ways (Lenz and Schneider 2002). Both share the common reference levels of language proficiency as a core element. These are reproduced as Document 1 in the Reference documents section of this book.

A wide range of portfolios have been produced in a number of European countries, and by transnational organizations. Because of the wide range of contexts they were drawn up for the portfolios often appear rather different. Nevertheless, they all share some fundamental principles. In particular:
- an ELP belongs in the hands of the learner—he/she is considered to be the owner of his/her ELP
- an ELP documents and gives value to all language and (inter-) cultural competences and experiences
- an ELP promotes plurilingualism and multiculturalism
- an ELP helps to develop learner autonomy.

In putting these principles into practice, every ELP has the double function of a learning companion, and a reporting and documentation tool.

The aim of ELPs is not only to support language users (including learners) who are already autonomous, but also to help to develop learner autonomy, including learner self-assessment.

Focus on the learner

Learner autonomy was a major concern of Council of Europe working groups in the 1980s and earlier. Publications by Henri Holec (autonomy) and Mats Oskarsson (self-assessment) were seminal in the field. Holec's definition of 'autonomy' as 'the ability to take charge of one's learning' (Holec 1981: 3) is still often cited. In his words this means for the learner to have, and to hold the responsibility for all the decisions concerning all aspects of this learning, i.e.
- determining the objectives
- defining the contents and progressions
- selecting methods and techniques to be used

- monitoring the procedure of acquisition properly speaking (rhythm, time, place, etc.)
- evaluating what has been acquired.

At the time, the case for learner autonomy had a strong political dimension, but since then it has become a widely accepted and promoted pedagogic principle and objective.

The Common European Framework sets out to be a basis for reflection and a common reference for 'practitioners of all kinds in the language field, including language learners themselves' (CEF: xi). The authors expect that adult learners who receive enough guidance and opportunities to decide on their learning in an institutional context are eventually able 'to make choices in respect of objectives, materials and working methods in the light of their own needs, motivations, characteristics and resources' (CEF: 142), and can then use the CEF to become aware of the options they have.

Guiding the learner through the CEF

One of the specialized user guides for the Framework, the 'Guide for Adult Learners', was written exactly for this target group of trained and highly independent learners (Bailly, Gremmo, and Riley, 2002). The authors list and discuss the relevant decisions that need to be taken at the different stages of the language learning process and point the learners to the relevant resources the CEF contains. The headings of the six chapters give a brief impression of the content of this guide:

Part 1 – Needs analysis
Part 2 – Comprehension and expression skills
Part 3 – Work organization
Part 4 – Methodology
Part 5 – Assessment
Part 6 – Learning styles

The authors of the CEF are realistic enough to know that proactive learners of this kind are still a rare species. Nevertheless, they consider that developing learner autonomy is a necessity because 'once teaching stops, further learning has to be autonomous' (CEF: 141). If lifelong learning is a reality, then 'learning to learn' needs to be an integral part of language instruction and learning (see also CEF: 144f.).

Portfolios and learner autonomy

Therefore, one important objective of the ELP is to promote learner autonomy, and to help to develop learning skills by providing suitable guidance and instruments for the learners themselves. The other main objective is to provide a pre-structured format that helps language users and learners to a document and present both their proficiency in all the languages they know (however much or little of them they know), and the extent of the intercultural knowledge and know-how they have acquired through different kinds of contact.

The three parts of the European Language Portfolio

In this section, the three-part structure of an ELP is briefly presented. The next section will show in more detail what elements each of the three parts may contain in order to put the intended functions of an ELP into practice.

Every European Language Portfolio must consist of three parts: Language Passport, Language Biography, and Dossier:

- The *Language Passport* gives an overview of the 'linguistic identity' and the current level of communicative language proficiency of its holder, and summarizes his/her learning and intercultural experiences.
- The *Language Biography* documents the personal history of language learning and intercultural experiences; it encourages reflection on these experiences in order to make them more fruitful. It also contains instruments for self-assessment of language proficiency and helps to plan (further) learning.
- The *Dossier* is a collection of documents of different kinds—mostly works produced by the learner him/herself—that have played some role in the learning process. Some ELPs distinguish between a Working Dossier and a Showcase Dossier. The Working Dossier accompanies daily language learning and documents the learning process, while the Showcase Dossier illustrates the present level of language proficiency, and possibly the state of intercultural knowledge and awareness, by means of concrete examples.

The roughly 50[1] different ELPs produced by over 20 different countries, regions, or transnational organizations that had been accredited by the end of 2003 vary considerably in appearance. It is obvious that ELPs for young children must be quite different from ELPs for adults; even at adult level, university students and migrants normally have different needs.

Some differences, however, cannot be explained by the characteristics of the target group. They concern features such as: the physical format (ring-binder, booklet, booklet plus 'treasure chest', etc.), the number and range of the instruments provided, the amount of written guidance for the learners/owners, the existence of supporting material for teachers, learners, and possibly other interested parties such as parents or employers.

Such a great diversity is possible because the guidelines for accreditation are still evolving. They are set out in *Principles and Guidelines* (Council of Europe 2001b) and the Council of Europe grants accreditation whenever these are followed.

Using a portfolio

As mentioned above, every ELP has a documentation and reporting function, as well as a pedagogic function. These functions are implemented in different ways and to varying degrees in the individual ELPs. This section gives an overview of elements that may be included in the three parts of the ELP to serve these functions. Because of my personal background, I will use the Swiss 'ELP for Young People and Adults' (Swiss ELP 15+) as a point of departure.[2]

The common reference levels

In virtually all ELPs the common reference levels are visible in the form of the 'Self-assessment Grid' in the Language Passport, and self-assessment checklists in the Language Biography. While the self-assessment checklists are often adapted to the needs of the learners that a specific ELP is designed for, the original grid (Document 2 in the Reference documents section of this book) has been made an obligatory

Peter Lenz

element of every ELP in order to prevent adaptations of the reference levels that would change them beyond recognition.

In ELPs for very young learners the grid is intended to inform adult users such as parents and teachers, about the complete system of levels, and to establish coherence with all other ELPs.

In the Swiss ELP 15+ the descriptors used in the grid and checklists are both directly based on descriptors from the CEF (Chapters 3–5, esp. 3.2–3.4). Most of these descriptors describe, in language which is easily understandable for users above the age of 14–15, relevant communication tasks language users are typically able to perform at various levels of language proficiency; other descriptors deal with qualitative aspects of the language produced, or with communication strategies.

The 'can do' formulations used in the CEF in order to define and illustrate the common levels had to be slightly adapted for the ELP: they were recast in an 'I can' format and often simplified, combined or cut apart in order to make them suitable for learner self-assessment. Some descriptors from the checklist for level A2 of the Swiss ELP 15+ may serve as an illustration of the final product:

Listening

- I can understand what is said clearly, slowly and directly to me in simple everyday conversation; it is possible to make me understand, if the speaker can take the trouble.
- I can generally identify the topic of discussion around me when people speak slowly and clearly.
- I can understand phrases, words and expressions related to areas of most immediate priority (e.g. very basic personal and family information, shopping, local area, employment).
- I can catch the main point in short, clear, simple messages and announcements.
- I can understand the essential information in short recorded passages dealing with predictable everyday matters which are spoken slowly and clearly.
- I can identify the main point of TV news items reporting events, accidents, etc. when the visual supports the commentary.

Language quality

- I can make myself understood using memorized phrases and single expressions.
- I can link groups of words with simple connectors like 'and', 'but' and 'because'.
- I can use some simple structures correctly.
- I have a sufficient vocabulary for coping with simple everyday situations.

In addition to Listening and Language quality set out above, Reading, Spoken interaction, and Spoken production, as well as Writing and Spoken interaction strategies, are described in this way. A more complete understanding of the skills and levels can be attained by actually going through the checklists of an ELP assessing one's own proficiency in (several) foreign languages.

Within the ELP the descriptors based on the reference levels link the different parts. The results of self-assessment are reported on the same scale and in the same terms as the results of assessment by others. (Self-)assessment can easily be linked with goal-setting and planning through descriptions that spell out in a concrete way what the next objectives in language learning could be. Little and Perclovà (2001) illustrate in their *Guide for Teachers and Teacher Trainers* how such an assessment-planning cycling can be applied in actual (school) practice.

The documentation and reporting function

One of the early motives for developing an ELP was to have a document that could bring together and make comparable all relevant evidence, both formal and informal, for a person's actual proficiency in all of his/her languages. The problem of comparability was crucial from the beginning. Experts working in the public school sector, in adult education, or in private enterprises, were often confronted with the fact that they could not interpret certificates, degrees, and diplomas in terms of actual language proficiency. Also, they did not feel they had appropriate means at hand to certify language proficiency attained formally or informally in their contexts. At the same time, person mobility had increased, and lifelong language learning had become a reality for many people, so that the need for a transparent and comparable measure had become quite urgent.

What instruments does the Swiss ELP 15+ provide in order to meet this demand?

Language Passport

The main answer to the reporting problem is the standardized 'Language Passport' booklet in A5 format, which is also a part of all other ELPs for adults. It consists of three main elements:

- a double page titled 'Profile of Language Skills' where learners can enter the results of their self-assessment of a maximum of six languages with respect to the five 'skills' of Listening, Reading, Spoken interaction, Spoken production and Writing. The self-assessment is based on proficiency descriptors that are calibrated against the six European reference levels. (See Figure 1.)

FIGURE 1 Specimen entry in the Language Passport, page 'Profile of Language Skills'. The entries for each of the five language skills/activities (see icons) are based on self-assessment. Six different levels of language proficiency are distinguished.

- two double-pages titled 'Summary of language learning and intercultural experiences' where information on course-based and informal language learning can be entered in a very concise form

- one double page where certificates and diplomas obtained can be entered; the learner also has the possibility to state the European level which each examination represents
- some of the authorities that included a Language Passport with their ELP, added extra 'soft' pages in order to suit their context better. ALTE, for example, the Association of Language Testers in Europe included a grid which gives information about the place of the awards issued by its members on the European six-level scale. In the Swedish ELP for upper-secondary students space was provided to list the levels reached within the official Swedish school system.

Together, these overviews are intended to provide a concise but still comprehensive picture of a person's language proficiency, and of their language learning and intercultural experience. A grid in the middle of the Passport booklet briefly describes for its users the six European reference levels for the five skills that are distinguished, and thus explains what the levels indicated in the 'Profile of Language Skills' and in the list of certificates actually mean in terms of language proficiency.

The Passport section of the Swiss ELP 15+ contains some additional documents which are intended to:
- facilitate self-assessment. Detailed level-specific self-assessment checklists are included.
- help to make examinations more transparent and more comparable. A form is provided that covers the relevant aspects of examinations, as well as a global scale which examination providers can use to roughly locate their examinations and grades on the European scale of levels.
- allow learners to provide evidence that backs up claims made in the booklet. Various 'attestation' forms are included on which learners can have their language and intercultural experiences certified.

Dossier and language biography

The dossier which contains personal work by a learner is another source of evidence to support claims made in the Passport, and is also used to make claims about skills and levels more tangible. Accounts of language learning and intercultural experiences in the Language Biography may serve a similar purpose.

Using the ELP with adults

An ELP which contains full details in every area may be too complex for some who want to make use of the ELP as a documentation and reporting tool; for other users it will be just right. One employer may be happy to know that an applicant speaks Italian at level B2, and has attained a corresponding certificate; for another employer (and a different kind of post) a rich repertoire of foreign languages, elaborate presentation skills in two or three languages, and extended experience in several countries may be crucial. A school-teacher will probably want to know more about the language background of a learner at the beginning of a three-year period of secondary schooling than the leader of a two-week holiday course. Therefore, the reporting instruments which the ELP provides need to be applied selectively by the learner.

When the ELP was launched in 2001, the Passport booklet was thought to be the basic instrument to be used for reporting. Meanwhile, experience has shown that many ELP users would like to have a one-page abstract of the most relevant information collected in the Language Passport. In order to meet this need, the Council of Europe is planning to provide an editable Passport Summary to download from its website.

Using the ELP with young learners

The reporting needs of young learners are usually very different from those of adults who are entering or have already entered a career. In the wider context of employment, the role of the common reference levels as defined in the CEF is certainly crucial because they help to identify existing skills in a transparent way, thus making them comparable. In the context of very young learners, maximum comparability by linking individual language proficiency to a widely known system of levels—developed for the world of adults—may not be relevant, and probably not even desirable.

However, if adapted to young learners, the reporting of skills and achievements in a transparent way can very well be useful, for example, to communicate objectives to the parents or to other teachers. Introducing descriptions of relevant language activities that learners are, or should be, able to do, may encourage the use of a task-based approach in the classroom, and may therefore be of great pedagogic value even if these descriptions do not correspond to the scaled descriptors of the CEF. *The Guide for Teachers and Teacher Trainers* (Little and Perclová 2001) discusses the pedagogic use of the ELP in a school context in more detail.

The question of whether a system of levels should be established especially for young learners up to the age of 11, and what it could look like, will be on the agenda for some years to come.

The pedagogic function

While all parts of the ELP may be considered to have a pedagogic function in one way or another, the Language Biography is the part that actually focuses on pedagogic aspects. It has three main aims:
- to encourage learners to have more language and intercultural contacts
- to motivate learners for more and better language learning
- to help learners to reflect on their language learning and intercultural experiences, plan effectively, and thereby move towards more self-direction, i.e. to become more autonomous learners.

Language biography sections in existing portfolios contain some or all of the following elements:
- personal, more or less detailed biographies, covering language learning, and sociocultural and intercultural experiences
- checklists for the self-assessment of language proficiency, and the setting of objectives related to the common reference levels
- instruments that help reflection on language learning experiences, and contacts with other cultures
- instruments that encourage learning from experience, or introduce effective working and learning methods, often building on reflection
- planning instruments such as lists of learning and language contact possibilities, lists of language learning objectives and worksheets for individual planning.

Peter Lenz

As a concrete example, the Language Biography part of the Swiss ELP 15+ contains the following elements:

- personal language learning biography—a worksheet which encourages learners to provide a chronological overview of their language learning and intercultural experiences. Learners are free to give an overview of their plurilingual and multicultural development as a whole, or to decide to write up a separate language learning biography for each language learned.
- self-assessment checklists—the detailed descriptions of language proficiency provided in these checklists may not only be used for self-assessment and assessment by others at a certain point in time; they may also be used to guide through the learning process, to identify and to set goals, and to assess one's learning progressively. The language proficiency descriptors may be complemented according to a learner's specific needs, for example, in the field of language learning for specific purposes.
- information about important linguistic and intercultural experiences—a worksheet that encourages learners to describe important experiences in more depth, such as contacts with speakers of other languages, learning about the cultural background of other languages, readings, and project work.
- information about foreign language teaching in schools and language courses—an instrument that helps to describe relevant aspects of course-based language teaching and learning. It is mainly intended for the use of teachers, language schools, and other educational institutions.
- my objectives—a worksheet that helps to formulate objectives and to make plans for language learning. In an environment of guided self-study, this sheet may take on the shape of a learning contract.

Different formats

The authors of the Swiss ELP 15+ chose to use an open form for most instruments in the Language Biography. An introductory text with prompts for reflection is usually followed by a blank space where the learners can note down their accounts, findings, and plans.

The ELP for lower secondary learners from North Rhine-Westphalia (Germany) complements instructions and prompts on otherwise empty pages with corresponding lists in the appendix that contain concrete examples and ideas. This design is used, for example, for the self-assessment of language skills and for the planning of language contacts.

In other ELPs, like those from Ireland, forms that pre-structure in detail the type and amount of information the learners are expected to provide, are used extensively for a wide range of purposes. For example, they may require the learner to list and reflect on observations concerning language and intercultural contacts, to reflect on communication strategies, and to draw up detailed work plans.

Some ELPs put special emphasis on features that are not present in others. The proficiency descriptors for teachers' classroom language in the Russian ELP for philologists, the checklists and reflection forms in the ELC (European Language Council) portfolio that prepares students in higher education for their stay in another country as part of the European mobility programme, and the learner-type questionnaires in the ELP from Lombardy may illustrate this point.

Effects beyond the individual

The ELP is designed as a companion for the individual language user and learner. However, if the ELP and/or the reference levels are not widely recognized in an area (or sector), its value as a reporting tool remains modest. But as soon as its use reaches a critical level it will not only be a more useful learning companion but may even bring about changes in educational planning and practice.

It is obvious that the ELP is not completely original in many respects. Its strength may lie in the fact that it bundles together and strengthens certain existing tendencies through its focus on language learners. Such tendencies are, for example:

- the development and recognition of plurilingual and intercultural competence
- collaboration between different teachers and subjects (different foreign languages, subjects taught using immersion approaches)
- bilingual teaching
- language learning outside school
- recognition of less well-known and less-taught languages
- task-based learning, teaching, and assessment
- self-directed learning
- self-assessment
- lifelong learning
- outcome-oriented syllabus planning, etc.

The 'subversive' potential of the ELP, the far-reaching changes in existing practice it may entail, is an aspect that makes the ELP a treasure chest for some people and a Trojan horse for others. The Swiss experience has shown that, whatever conclusion is reached, the ELP raises the interest of many of those working in language professions.

Notes

1 For an updated overview see www.coe.int/portfolio > Portfolios.

2 The forms and worksheets from the Swiss ELP 15+ can be downloaded in five languages, including English, from the Swiss ELP website (www.languageportfolio.ch> ELP 15+ > Learners > Downloads). The explanatory texts are only available in the printed version of that ELP. A French and English version of the standardised Language Passport can be downloaded from the Council of Europe ELP website (www.coe.int/portfolio> Introduction > '3 Parts of a Portfolio').

References

Bailly, S., M-J. Gremmo, and **P. Riley.** 2002. 'Guide for Adult Learners' in Council of Europe (ed.). *Common European Framework of Reference for Languages, Learning, teaching, assessment. A Guide for Users:* 47–71. Strasbourg: Council of Europe. Online: www.coe.int/portfolio> Documentation ('Supporting Documents').

Holec, H. 1981. *Autonomy and Foreign Language Learning.* Oxford: Pergamon.

Council of Europe. 2001a. *Common European Framework of Reference for Languages: Learning, teaching, assessment.* Cambridge: Cambridge University Press.

Council of Europe. 2001b. *Principles and Guidelines.*
Online: www.coe.int/portfolio > Documentation
('Key Documents').

Lenz, P. and G. Schneider. 2002. 'Developing the
Swiss Model of the European Language Portfolio' in
*Common European Framework of Reference for
Languages: Learning, teaching, assessment. Case
Studies:* 68–86. Strasbourg: Council of Europe.
Online: www.coe.int/portfolio> Documentation
('Other Documents').

Little, D. and R. Perclovà. 2001. *Guide for Teachers
and Teacher Trainers.* Strasbourg: Council of Europe.
Online: www.coe.int/portfolio> Documentation
('Key Documents').

Oskarsson, M. 1978. *Approaches to Self-Assessment in
Foreign Language Learning* Strasbourg: Council of
Europe

**Schneider, G., B. North, L. Koch, Swiss Conference of
Cantonal Ministers of Education.** (ed.). 2001.
*European Language Portfolio for Young People and
Adults.* Bern: Schulverlag blmv. Online:
http://www.languageportfolio.ch> ELP Model 15+.

The author

Peter Lenz is a lecturer in German as a Foreign
Language at the University of Fribourg,
Switzerland, and co-author of the *Guide for
Developers* of European Language Portfolios. He is a
member of the Validation Committee for ELPs of
the Council of Europe, and a member of the ELP
steering committee of the Swiss Conference of
Cantonal Ministers of Education.

Learning to learn with the CEF

Luciano Mariani

Overview

In the past few decades learning, including language learning, has increasingly been seen not just as the accumulation of sets of fixed items of knowledge, but also as the ability to change, adapt, and update these items according to both the needs of the individual learner, and the requirements of the contexts in which knowledge needs to be used.

Several factors have contributed to this change of perspective, including, among others, the very rapid rate of change in knowledge itself, due to scientific and technological advances, and the corresponding need for flexible uses of knowledge, both in the labour market and in society at large (European Communities 1995; Council of Europe 2000).

In a constantly changing world, the ability to put one's resources to a variety of uses, including uses which were not practised, or even foreseen, when one first acquired or developed those resources early in life, is gradually coming to be considered an essential feature of learning—not just formal learning in educational institutions, but also informal learning arising from both professional and personal experience. In other words, learning no longer belongs exclusively to an early stage in life, but includes the ability to adapt and change throughout one's lifespan. Lifelong education implies not just learning, but learning how to learn. (For a comprehensive bibliography on lifelong learning and related issues, see Eurydice 2000.)

The ability to learn in the Common European Framework

In Chapter 5.1, the CEF 2001 recognizes that the ability to learn (also referred to as 'savoir-apprendre', or 'knowing how to learn') is part of the general competences of a language user or language learner:

> In its most general sense, 'savoir-apprendre' is the ability to observe and participate in new experiences and to incorporate new knowledge into existing knowledge, modifying the latter where necessary. (CEF 2001: 106)

Learning to learn languages

As such, the ability to learn is not part of the user's/learner's communicative language competences, because it is of more general relevance to all kinds of learning. However, the CEF breaks it down into four areas which are of more direct interest for language learning:

1 Language and communication awareness, or becoming aware of what languages are, how they work, how they are used, how they can be learnt and taught.

2 General phonetic awareness and skills, or being able to discriminate and articulate sounds (as a general skill, not with reference to a specific language).

3 Study skills, or being able to use the learning opportunities offered by teaching contexts. This encompasses a very wide range of abilities, from cognitive, e.g. maintaining attention, grasping the intention of a task, developing a language repertoire by observing and participating in communicative events, to social, e.g. co-operating in class, to more general psychological features, e.g. becoming aware of one's strengths and weaknesses, identifying one's own goals, organizing one's strategies, also making use of independent or self-directed learning opportunities.

4 Heuristic skills, or being able to use new experience by applying higher-order cognitive operations (like analysing, inferencing, memorizing, etc.); and being able to find and use new information (including the use of information and communication technologies).

Thus the CEF suggests that the ability to learn can be seen as a very general competence, mainly focused on the ability to face the challenge of the new, whether new languages, new people, or new cultural issues. At the same time, it can be broken down into several more specific components.

Apart from the general phonetic skills, which may be seen to belong to a rather specific aspect of language competence, the other components refer to very broad areas of a person's general competences, so that we could say that the picture of 'learning to learn' emerging from the CEF implies three different (although closely related) areas:

- developing a wide range of skills
- acquiring knowledge about the process of learning
- discovering a set of personal beliefs and attitudes towards the experience of learning itself.

Complexity

It is a very complex picture, but we need to retain and value this complexity in order to fully grasp what is involved in perhaps the greatest challenge facing (language) learners today—their ability to learn how to learn. Such ability comes as the fourth and last component of the general competences identified by the CEF in Chapter 5.1, but, as we shall soon see, it encompasses the other three components: it cuts across skills and know-how ('savoir-faire', or knowing how to do things), declarative knowledge ('savoir', or knowing things) and existential competence ('savoir-être', or 'knowing how to be').

The questions we shall address in the remainder of this chapter will therefore be:

- how can we better identify and further illustrate the three areas we have just identified?
- what can a more careful consideration of the learning to learn issue imply for learning and teaching a language?

Learning to learn as skills development

Although the lists of skills provided by the CEF as part of the 'ability to learn' competence include areas such as the more traditional reference skills (like using a dictionary or a grammar book) or the more recent audiovisual and computer skills, the emphasis is clearly on more demanding cognitive operations or mental processes. More practical illustrations of examples mentioned by the CEF might include:

- using inference to guess the meaning of unknown words; or, more broadly speaking, inferring meaning from a written text or a piece of oral interaction by filling in the gaps in one's knowledge through the use of contextual clues and background information
- using directed and selected attention to focus on specific aspects of the language input, or 'noticing' what is new in the input, and adding it to one's own language repertoire, thus learning from observation and experience
- using an inductive approach to formulate language 'rules' by comparing examples of language use, and making appropriate generalizations
- memorizing linguistic and cultural items by using a range of techniques, e.g. by classifying items into meaningful sets or categories.

Metacognitive skills

However, the same lists of skills also include what we might call metacognitive operations, or reflecting on (and so becoming more aware of) one's own learning. This process of reflection can cover the full range of operations required in planning, monitoring, and evaluating a learning experience, e.g.

- establishing one's own needs and goals in language learning
- choosing long-, medium- and short-term objectives, e.g. from establishing a desired level of competence to be reached within a certain deadline, to planning what textbook exercises to do during a week
- choosing the most appropriate resources (materials, activities, opportunities) to reach those objectives
- identifying problems in the process of using or learning the language, e.g. by asking oneself questions to check comprehension while listening or reading; by checking if one's message has been understood in oral interaction; by using a grid to keep written production under control
- self-assessing, both the results, i.e. the product or outcome of learning, and the ways and means used in the experience, i.e. the process of learning. It is interesting that the CEF does not explicitly mention self-assessment as a specific component of the ability to learn.

Skills or strategies?

Many of the examples provided above as learning to learn 'skills' are often mentioned in the foreign language literature, as well as in textbooks, as 'strategies', so that teachers and students often talk about cognitive and metacognitive strategies, social or affective strategies, compensation or communication strategies as part of a learning to learn approach. This rather confusing picture is acknowledged by the CEF itself, which does not aim to provide either a definitive interpretation of the issue or an alternative way of considering it:

Luciano Mariani

The word 'strategies' has been used in different ways. Here what is meant is the adoption of a particular line of action in order to maximise effectiveness.
(CEF 2001: 57)

By adopting a rather 'loose' definition of strategies, the CEF manages to accommodate several meanings of the term, and several corresponding applications. Strategies are not seen to belong to the user/learner's general or communicative language competences but come into play in the context of using language in communicative language activities:

Strategies are a means the language user exploits to mobilise and balance his or her resources, to activate skills and procedures, in order to fulfil the demands of communication in context and successfully complete the task in question in the most comprehensive or most economical way feasible depending on his or her precise purpose.
(CEF 2001: 57)

This means that strategies are seen as a sort of a bridge between the learner's competences and the demands of the communicative situation. In other words, although strategies clearly draw on the learner's personal knowledge and know-how, their use is called upon only in the context of actual communicative activities, especially when the learner experiences a problem which cannot be solved through routine behaviour.

Thus strategies seem to possess a higher status than simple tactics, techniques, or 'recipes' for learning, because they often imply the activation of higher-order, complex operations in the cognitive, social and affective realms, and some degree of conscious choice (Cohen 1998; Kasper and Kellerman 1997).

Strategies in the CEF To find examples of strategies in the CEF, one therefore needs to refer to the lists and descriptors of communicative language activities in Chapter 4.4, within which they have been accommodated. This establishes a direct link between the two concepts, e.g.

- in oral and written production (speaking and writing), learners can find themselves in situations where they have to adjust the task or the message so that it can fit their actual present level of competence. For example, they may decide to write a postcard rather than a letter; to shorten or simplify a stretch of discourse; to content themselves with a generic expression of their thoughts and feelings rather than aim at being more detailed and specific. They may need to find ways of compensating the gaps in their linguistic and communicative competence by using gestures and facial expressions, by using more general words ('flower' instead of 'geranium'), by defining or describing a person or an object instead of using the exact word ('it's a person who cuts people's hair'; 'it's a machine that you use to keep the air cool').
- in aural and visual reception (listening and reading), too, learners may need to compensate for gaps in their competence, for example by using the overall meaning of a text, as well as their familiarity with the topic, to guess the meaning of unknown words. They may also concentrate on specific details or main points in order to establish a

clear purpose for listening to or reading a complex text. They may stop at regular intervals while reading a text to check the hypotheses they have been making, and perhaps revise them in light of the information contained in a later paragraph.

- in spoken and written interaction, learners may need to ask for clarification, for example, by simply saying that they didn't follow, or by asking for repetition, or to speak more slowly. They may decide to repeat what they have just heard to obtain confirmation from their interlocutor; to ask how to say something; to ask if they have been understood. Learners may also help to 'keep the conversation going', for example by showing interest, encouraging others to talk, using fillers or stock phrases to gain time and carry on the interaction.

Although the CEF provides a theoretical framework for strategies and lists of general strategy categories for each communicative language activity, it does not set out to provide a wide range of examples for each category. This is probably because it has clearly proved to be a very demanding (if not impossible) task to provide illustrative scales for strategies for the six CEF levels of competence (A1 to C2). If we consider, for example, a strategy category like 'asking for clarification', it is quite difficult to say which concrete strategies can be considered as typical of a learner at, say, A2 rather than B1 level.

However, the concept of 'strategies', has proved to be quite productive, and it is certainly useful to continue making them part of a learning to learn programme, even if only a few detailed illustrative scales are available at the moment. As long as their role in language learning and teaching is made clear to both learners and teachers, it makes sense to encourage learners to explore, find out and use strategies—not just for the short-term effect of solving a specific problem in a specific task, but for the more general, long-term goal of educating them to become more responsible and independent in their language learning experiences (Weaver and Cohen 1997; Uhl Chamot et al. 1999).

Learning to learn as information acquisition and attitude discovery

Skills and strategies are closely integrated with declarative knowledge of different kinds which have a direct impact on the overall ability to learn. Examples of this knowledge provided in the CEF are:

> knowledge of what morpho-syntactical relations correspond to given declension patterns ... or awareness that there may be a taboo or particular rituals associated with dietary or sexual practices in certain cultures ...
> (CEF 2001: 12)

Knowing about language learning

However, such examples of knowledge of the world and sociocultural knowledge do not limit the kinds of information that it is useful for learners to acquire and become aware of, especially in relation to those areas which are of more direct relevance for their own process of language learning, such as:

- the nature of language, communication and culture, e.g. what is a language? How is it used as a formal system, as a social tool for communication and as a vehicle for cultural meanings?

- the learning and teaching of languages, e.g. how can a language be learnt and taught? What facilitates these processes? What roles should be played by learners and teachers in this respect?
- their cognitive, social and affective profile as language learners, e.g. how do personal attitudes, preferences, personality factors, learning styles, and motivations affect learning experiences?
- the features of the tasks which they have to carry out both in learning and in using a language, e.g. what are the specific task demands in terms of knowledge and competences? What kinds of procedures should be gone through? What level of difficulty can be expected, and how could possible problems be solved?

Such areas of knowledge are not listed as such in the CEF, but some of them are clearly mentioned as illustrations of the learner's 'existential competence', which is defined as:

> the sum of the individual characteristics, personality traits and attitudes which concern, for example, self-image and one's view of others and willingness to engage with other people in social interaction.
> (CEF 2001: 11)

Once again, it is clear that the various kinds of general competences identified by the CEF are often bound to overlap, especially when one considers a very general and comprehensive concept as personal identity (which includes one's identity as a language learner).

Beliefs and attitudes   Although beliefs and attitudes are simply mentioned by the CEF as illustrations of existential competence, it is useful to give them special consideration, since they are the basic factors which affect decision-making.

What learners think and how learners feel about the various areas of knowledge listed above are of crucial importance for their actual performance in language learning and language use. In other words, the decisions that learners make and the actions they perform with respect to their language learning experience are affected, to a considerable degree, by their hidden curriculum and their hidden agenda, their often unconscious and rarely explored ideas of language, learning and their role in the process (Wenden 1986; Wenden 1991; Woods 1996).

Consider for example what is involved in carrying out a communicative activity like 'Can recognize significant points in straightforward newspaper articles on familiar subjects', a descriptor for one of the reading activities at B1 level. Many teachers would label the skill involved in this activity as skimming, or reading for gist or main points. If learners wanted to develop and/or use their ability to learn in connection with this communicative activity, what would they need to know, be able to do, and be ready to be?

Depending on the level of the linguistic-communicative competences they can already rely on, strategies may be called for, for example, to 'identify unfamiliar words from the context' or to 'extrapolate the meaning of occasional unknown words and deduce sentence meaning'—

two strategies explicitly listed in the only illustrative scale provided by the CEF for reception strategies (CEF 2001: 72).

However, learners actually use (and teachers actually teach) a wide range of strategies which would be useful in such a reading task: focusing on the headings and sub-headings of the article; considering features like words printed in bold or in italics; recalling the features typical of the text type under consideration; examining photographs and their captions if they are available; making a list of what they know about the topic; and so on.

Individual differences

However, not all these strategies are useful to all learners in the same way; indeed, learners can make effective use of strategies only to the extent that they can be accommodated within their personal learning preferences and, in particular, cognitive style. For instance, while 'global, random, intuitive' learners may find themselves relatively at ease with a skimming task (a global comprehension activity), and may encounter fewer problems and need less strategy activation, 'analytic, sequential, systematic' learners may find more problems and may therefore be helped by a more explicit, consistent, and conscious use of appropriate strategies.

In the same way, visually-oriented people may take more advantage of the graphic features of the text and its layout than auditory-oriented people. This means that a knowledge of the factors affecting communicative activities (in this case, cognitive styles, mentioned by the CEF as existential competence), and a personal awareness of one's learning preferences have a direct impact on the way tasks are carried out, and on how the relevant ability to learn is developed and/or used.

However, the use of strategies in this reading task is also affected by the beliefs that learners hold with respect to what 'reading' means to them, and by the corresponding attitude (or affective-motivational response) that is inextricably linked with their belief.

Making use of many of the strategies mentioned above implies that learners somehow believe (or are at least willing to 'suspend their disbelief') that, for example, there are various ways to read a text depending on the type of text and the reading purpose; that for certain purposes one does not need to understand every single word; that what a reader brings to the text, in terms of her/his previous knowledge and experience, is just as important as what the text brings to the reader. And, in connection with all this, learners also need to 'feel' that they are willing to take reasonable risks, which in turn implies that they are prepared to tolerate ambiguity, and the anxiety that is involved in not being able to understand several, or perhaps many, of the words and sentences in a text.

Here again, an awareness of the beliefs and attitudes (mentioned by the CEF as 'existential competence') held by learners with respect to what is involved in learning, and an awareness of the features of their personal profile as (language) learners, can considerably affect the way learners can develop and use their ability to learn.

Luciano Mariani

Implications for learning and teaching

The CEF does not set out to recommend any specific approach to learning and teaching languages, but rather aims to provide a frame of reference within which learners and teachers can make informed choices. For example, the CEF describes a range of options for the treatment of existential competence, which may be:

a ignored as the learner's personal concern
b taken into account in planning and monitoring the learning process
c included as an objective of the learning programme.
(CEF 2001: 149)

In the same way, it is stated that areas such as study skills, heuristic skills, and the responsibility for one's own learning can be treated in a variety of ways, from 'considering them simply as "spin-off" from language learning and teaching, without any special planning or provision' to 'getting learners to recognise their own cognitive style and to develop their own learning strategies accordingly'. (CEF 2001: 149)

One could therefore argue that by leaving users free to choose from a full range of methodological options, the CEF does not directly encourage explicit and systematic actions in the areas which we have put forward as essential components of an ability to learn, i.e. strategies development, information acquisition, and belief/attitude discovery. However, one cannot forget the long-standing commitment of the Council of Europe to promoting learner autonomy and the emphasis on helping learners to learn how to learn. In fact, elsewhere the CEF clearly mentions the usefulness, indeed the necessity, of promoting autonomy through the development of an ability to learn:

Autonomous learning can be promoted if 'learning to learn' is regarded as an integral part of language learning, so that learners become increasingly aware of the way they learn, the options open to them and the options that best suit them. (CEF 2001: 141)

Learning to learn as part of a teaching programme

In light of such a position, one can legitimately claim that a concern with empowering students by developing their ability to learn should form part of a teaching programme, although its implementation may take a variety of forms. Indeed, for the past few decades teachers' practices and teaching materials have often included opportunities for students to deal with various aspects of their ability to learn. Broadly speaking, these opportunities can be seen as belonging to two distinct methodological approaches.

A discrete point approach
Here one or more areas are dealt with in relative isolation. Practical examples of this approach are:
- study skills courses offered alongside the main language lessons
- materials devoted to specific skills or strategies, like using a dictionary, note-taking, or finding information on the Internet
- questionnaires on learning styles, learning strategies, or multiple intelligences
- surveys and interviews inviting students to express and share their opinions about teaching materials and techniques

- 'language awareness' projects
- activities aimed at making students (and teachers) more aware of their needs, beliefs, attitudes, and motivations, towards language learning, often used in the introductory parts of courses and textbooks.

An integrated approach

In this approach, the various components of an ability to learn are woven, so to speak, into the learners' overall experience of language learning, so that an element of reflection and awareness is built into the learning tasks. Tasks themselves are then considered as the 'raw material' for strategies development, information acquisition, and attitude discovery. The approach is more often than not explicit, experiential, embedded and evaluative, because students are directly invited to consider strategies, beliefs, and attitudes in the context of what they are doing, as an integral part of their planning, execution, and evaluation of tasks. An example of an activity based on this approach can be found in the Appendix to this chapter.

The two approaches are complementary rather than mutually exclusive, and in practice teachers and teaching materials often use both, in a range of ways, depending on the features of their own educational contexts. Incidentally, one may also consider this flexibility as perhaps the main message carried by the above-mentioned quotations from the CEF.

Beyond the variety of ways in which an ability to learn can be promoted, however, lies the value of reflection and awareness-raising in helping students to realize their own strengths and weaknesses, thus increasing their level of self-regulation and, in the long term, their capacity to act as more independent (language) learners.

References

European Communities. 1995. *White Paper on Education and Training: Teaching and Learning—Towards the Learning Society.* Luxembourg: Office for Official Publications of the European Communities.

Eurydice. 2000. *Lifelong Learning—Thematic bibliography.* Brussels: Eurydice, the information network on education in Europe.

Council of Europe. 2000. *Lifelong Learning for Equity and Social Cohesion: A New Challenge to Higher Education: Progress Report.* Strasbourg: Council of Europe.

Cohen, A. D. 1998. *Strategies in Learning and Using a Second Language.* Harlow: Longman.

Council of Europe. 2001. *Common European Framework of Reference for Languages: Learning, Teaching, Assessment.* Cambridge: Cambridge University Press. Also available for download from http://www.coe.int/T/E/Cultural_Co-operation/education/Languages/Language_Policy/Common_Framework_of_Reference/1cadre.asp#TopOfPage

Kasper, G. and **E. Kellerman.** (eds.). 1997. *Communication Strategies. Psycholinguistic and Sociolinguistic Perspectives.* Harlow: Longman.

Mariani, L. and **G. Pozzo.** 2002. *Stili, Strategie e Strumenti nell'Apprendimento Linguistico: Imparare a Imparare, Insegnare a Imparare.* Firenze: RCS—La Nuova Italia, Collana LEND.

Uhl Chamot, A., S. Barnhardt, P. Beard El-Dinary, and **J. Robbins.** 1999. *The Learning Strategies Handbook.* White Plains: Addison-Wesley Longman.

Weaver, S. J. and **A. D. Cohen.** 1997. *Strategies-Based Instruction: A Teacher-Training Manual.* Minneapolis: University of Minnesota, Center for Advanced Research on Language Acquisition.

Wenden, A. 1986. 'Helping language learners think about learning'. *ELT Journal* 40/1: 3–12.

Wenden, A. 1991. *Learner Strategies for Learner Autonomy.* Hemel Hempstead: Prentice-Hall.

Woods, D. 1996. *Teacher Cognition in Language Teaching.* Cambridge: Cambridge University Press.

Luciano Mariani

The author

Luciano Mariani is a freelance consultant, teacher trainer, and materials writer based in Milan, Italy. He has published widely on the topics of study skills, learning styles and strategies, and learner autonomy, and is the author of cross-curricular materials such as *Study Skills through English, Strategie per Imparare and Portfolio,* published by Zanichelli, Bologna. He runs a web site (www.learningpaths.org), in Italian and English, which is specifically devoted to learner education and teacher development.

Appendix
(from Mariani and
Pozzo 2002)

This activity was originally designed for adolescent students (age range 14–15), studying English as a Foreign Language in a state secondary school in Italy, who were approximately at A2 level and had just started working towards B1 level. Their former experience of 'learning to learn' was very limited or non-existent, and they exhibited a remarkable level of anxiety when faced with listening tasks.

The activity therefore tried to address both the issue of strategy training and the issue of raising the students' awareness of their beliefs and attitudes towards listening tasks in the classroom, including their affective reactions. The short 'before listening' questionnaire was designed to make them verbalize and share their thoughts and feelings, while at the same time introducing some 'positive strategies' (the pair and class discussion was conducted in the students' mother tongue, i.e. Italian). This proved to be an effective way of lowering the anxiety level and preparing students to approach the task in a more relaxed way. After listening, the teacher summarized the problems and strategies experienced by the students on a poster, which was systematically referred to and updated during later listening tasks.

In this way, the students showed a gradual increase in their confidence towards listening tasks as well as in their capacity to self-regulate their strategy use.

Task

Listen to three short conversations in which Simon and Julie express some personal opinions. For each conversation try to understand
a what they are talking about
b if their opinions are positive or negative
c what more specific comments they make.

Before listening

Read what these students do when they listen to conversations in an English class. Do you do the same? What seems most useful to you? Tick (✓) your choices, then compare them with a classmate.

Do you do the same?		What seems most useful to you?
☐	I try to understand every single word.	☐
☐	I read the task instructions carefully to check what exactly I have to understand.	☐
☐	I immediately get anxious and think I won't understand anything.	☐
☐	I pay attention to the different tones of voice and background noises.	☐
☐	I get stuck if I miss something.	☐
☐	I carry on listening and try to put together the bits that I understand.	☐

After listening

Discuss with your classmates and your teacher:
■ Did you have problems in this task? What caused them?
■ How did you cope with the problems? What helped you?

Luciano Mariani

The CEF and the secondary school syllabus

Julia Starr Keddle

Overview

Working with the CEF in secondary schools, I have come to believe that it is an essential tool for the 21st century. However, I find that I am both an enthusiast and a critic.

Some advantages of the CEF are its renewed focus on situational and functional language, and on the strategies students need in the four skills, especially oral skills. There is also a focus on learner language and a move away from mechanical grammar work, which contributes to more communicative language practice. One of the great strengths of the CEF is the accompanying Language Portfolio, as this promotes self-assessment, autonomy, and continuity across school levels and into the real world.

However, there are challenges in using the CEF in schools. It doesn't measure grammar-based progression, and this creates a barrier between the descriptors and the students' achievements. It is also not necessarily suited to school-based learners, and the necessary adaptation creates work. The individual self-assessment descriptors are not exhaustive: some accepted concept areas are not covered, and some functional areas are not there at all. The work involved in using and understanding the CEF creates barriers to its widespread application in the school classroom.

Introduction

In developing and writing materials for teaching 11–16 year olds, particularly in Italy, I have been working with aspects of the CEF for over five years. I started by integrating the CEF into pre-existing courses (effectively matching the stated objectives of the course with the descriptors). This was a time of familiarization with this new tool, understanding how it worked, and relating the CEF to pre-existing syllabus elements.

Focus

Because of the way the CEF has been distributed and used within Italy, the documents that are commonly used are the global descriptors, and the self-assessment checklist 'can do' statements. (See Documents 1 and 2 in the Reference documents section of this book.) The use of the checklists is a backwash effect from European Language Portfolio work (see the chapter by Peter Lenz in this collection), which has been integrated more quickly into Italian language education than the CEF package as a whole. Most of my references in this chapter will be to the 'can do' statements, and do not necessarily focus on the more global way in which the CEF can be used for curriculum design.

Approaches to the CEF
Integrating CEF with pre-existing courses

The integration of the CEF with pre-existing courses was problematic, not least because of the mismatch between the checklists and the standard, accepted, grammar syllabus progression in secondary school classrooms. The global descriptors fit any successful language learning situation, including the school classroom, but the detailed descriptors often don't match with the grammar focus found at school level.

It is common for teachers to discuss the order of tense presentation and measure student progress by their mastery of grammar areas. They may speak about having 'done' the past simple or 'doing' the present perfect, and while other strands such as functions, skills, pronunciation, etc. are covered, the foundation of much classroom work is grammatical.

Working with self-assessment descriptors and existing syllabuses, I have become increasingly frustrated by the clash between existing 'accepted' syllabuses and the aims of the CEF, which are based on achievements in communicative competencies, strategies, discourse recognition, and performance in everyday situational/functional areas. Adding CEF objectives *after* the main syllabus strands have been established only works up to a point. Even the standard functional areas taught by most of the teachers I meet don't necessarily 'match' with the self-assessment descriptors of the CEF.

Starting from scratch

Consequently I have decided to design CEF-based syllabuses from scratch. But I am afraid of 'throwing out the baby with the bath water'. I don't want to turn upside down a working model which teachers are relatively happy with and replace it with something unworkable. I am interested in preparing a syllabus and developing activities that truly reflect both the CEF and the tried and tested grammar strands. So I am planning a syllabus that is 'led' by both specific grammatical structures and the CEF.

It is not an easy process, and has a lot of loose ends, but it is certainly more effective to work with the CEF at the beginning of the planning process, because it feeds into both the macro 'curriculum planning' level and the micro 'classroom level' work. But it doesn't feel radical, and it surely shouldn't be. After all, the CEF is an analysis of what we actually do with languages, and tries to define objectively what distinguishes a beginner from an intermediate or advanced user of the language. Surely that is the starting point for language courses, teaching programmes, and course books too? And if we want to unite these two 'cultural monuments' (and I mean that positively)—the syllabus and CEF—then we need to do so at the beginning of the planning process.

I want now to outline what I consider to be the advantages and disadvantages of working with the CEF, and then conclude by showing an example of a plan for a unit of work, and an extract from a syllabus.

Julia Starr Keddle

Some advantages of using CEF in the school classroom
Focus on situational/function language

The CEF focuses on what you *do* with language—it is out in the real world and distant from the unnatural habitat of the classroom. For example, in A1 we have 'asking people for things', making simple purchases', 'describing where I live'; and in A2 'using public transport', 'ordering food and drink', etc.

Although situational/functional language is a strand in school language programmes, grammar-based planning has been favoured in recent years. Functions are often found in a list of objectives, but when you come to look for them, they are often sidelined to a corner of a page, or divorced from the main teaching materials, particularly for younger learners. The CEF emphasis on functional/situational language use allows us to revisit this area, and bring the real world back into the classroom.

Focus on skills and strategies

In the late 1970s and early 1980s the skills and strategies students use when reading, writing, speaking, and listening were often taught through specific materials, treating the interaction between the student and authentic texts as a communicative act (see for example Coe, Rycroft, and Ernest 1983). They encouraged students to recognize that they had skills in their L1 which they could transfer into L2.

Since the arrival of mega-coursebooks and the decline in use of supplementary material, this approach has often been downplayed. The CEF, with its references to text types (e.g. news summaries, messages, advertisements, instructions, questionnaires, and signs), provides teachers with a checklist they can use to incorporate genuine communicative skills/strategies work into their teaching. Authentic text-types can be adapted to suit the interests and age level of students, and clear objectives can be set to fit their language level such as these descriptors for A2:

> 'I can skim small advertisements in newspapers'
> 'I can catch the main point in short clear simple messages and announcements'.

Focus on learner language

Although teachers are aware of theories of language acquisition, they still tend to measure student performance against a native-speaker, error-free absolute, even at beginner levels. 'Factual' areas such as vocabulary or grammar may be tested with exercises that have one 'correct' answer, so that no distinction is made between a beginner or advanced student.

In the CEF, on the other hand, the language user's performance is described in terms of what they can be expected to achieve at a particular level relative to the hours they have studied a language, and the average way in which a student at that level performs. If we take Listening, we can see the way the expectations are raised at successive levels. The student is expected at:

> Level A1: to understand 'when someone speaks slowly to me'

> Level A2: to understand 'what is said clearly, slowly and directly to me in simple everyday conversation'

Level B1: to be able to 'follow clearly articulated speech directed at me in everyday conversation'

Level B2: to 'understand in detail what is said to me in standard spoken language, even in a noisy environment'.

This graded description and measurement of performance moves away from the use of simplified, inauthentic materials and brings the focus back to the difficulty of the task. It allows teachers and students to describe performance at any level, even the most basic, and show progress.

The emphasis through all the levels of the CEF is on 'getting by' in a language, although accuracy becomes progressively more significant as you go up the levels. In the lower levels in particular, where most of the work I do focuses, the descriptors define practical achievements.

Consequently, we find qualifiers such as:

A1: 'I am dependent on my partner being prepared to repeat more slowly and rephrase what I say to help me say what I want'

A2: 'I can understand what is said clearly ... if the speaker can take the trouble'

B1: 'I can maintain a conversation but may sometimes be difficult to follow.'

I believe that this is a welcome change of direction, especially for secondary schools—where the emphasis is often on accurate but limited and unnatural communication. The descriptors allow an 'imperfect' performance to be appropriate for someone of that level, rather than being perceived as a failure. The provision of checklists that make this type of performance clear to students should be reassuring for them, accustomed as they are to being marked down for 'mistakes', and such lists give the teacher a clear description of student performance.

Because the CEF also identifies communication strategies (asking someone to repeat what they said, asking someone to clarify, keeping a conversation going, or taking turns, etc.), the teacher and students are encouraged to develop competences which greatly enhance communication, but which can easily be overlooked in the language classroom.

Less focus on mechanical grammar practice

The self-assessment descriptors, quite deliberately, do not refer to grammar or structures. They speak about how you communicate, and how well you understand text and speech—the grammar used is a part of your performance of the task.

If you demonstrate that you 'can listen to a short narrative and form hypotheses about what will happen next' (B1), you are clearly using grammar and structure to achieve this objective. While an English teacher would infer that 'narrating' will involve understanding of past forms, and possibly some reported speech, and that hypothesizing about 'what will happen next' involves future forms and modality, the descriptors do not prescribe what structures should be used. The CEF

Julia Starr Keddle

puts the emphasis on what you achieve with grammar, providing only a framework for curriculum decisions:

> The Framework cannot replace reference grammars or provide a strict ordering (though scaling may involve selection and hence some ordering in global terms) but provides a framework for the decisions of practitioners to be made known.
> (CEF 2001: 152)

This move away from grammar and into competences allows a true comparison to be made between performance in different European languages, as there is no need to find grammar equivalency. Students can define their performance in terms of the CEF levels, and find correspondence with students with different L1s and different target languages.

However, this 'framework' approach creates a lot of difficulties as well, and while the lack of grammar 'landmarks' is without doubt a great strength of the CEF, it also causes problems in planning, as I discuss later.

Links between student achievements and external exams

Exams such as those from Cambridge ESOL and Trinity College London define what CEF levels you need to attain in order to take their exams successfully. Indeed, a lot of CEF descriptors match well with the communicative skills required by these exams. A curriculum that is based on the framework, with its focus on communicative competences, can help to ensure that students are developing appropriate exam skills, such as looking at authentic text types and performing real-world communicative acts.

For example, descriptors from the self-assessment checklist such as 'I can understand the main points in short newspaper articles about current and familiar topics' (B1) or 'I can write short simple notes and messages' (A2) harmonize with the requirements of the Cambridge PET exam, and a course based around such descriptors allows teachers to spend more time on the general language programme, and less time on specific exam preparation.

Self-assessment and autonomy

The CEF offers a 'package' for the student and teacher. If the school programme is designed to reflect CEF levels and the single descriptors, then work with the Portfolio becomes much easier to administer and more streamlined. Students will find that they have been doing tasks that they can then tick off in the Portfolio self-assessment checklist. This will give them a sense of achievement because they find that what they are studying is clearly linked to the Portfolio. It is a way of making sense of the sometimes wordy language of the descriptors, and gives the students something portable that they can use in their future careers.

Another positive spin-off from the CEF guidelines is the emphasis on study skills and overall educational competences which can help students to become better language learners, encouraging them to become language learners for life, and not simply when they are at school.

The self-assessment checklist can also be helpful in relation to remedial work. If a student's pronunciation makes him/her an A1 speaker while he/she continues to progress into A2 or B1 in the other skills, he/she will be able to see this clearly and neutrally when completing the checklists, and know where to focus remedial action.

Encouragement of continuity

By giving students ownership of their performance, and giving teachers descriptors which are transferable, there should be a backwash effect, where A1 level students arriving from one school cannot be treated as beginners again. As the descriptors describe the competences of the students in terms of fluency, teachers may be led away from simply testing grammar and vocabulary knowledge. They may instead prefer to confirm the students' attested level through assessment that reflects the nature of an A1 user. This can allow the students to consolidate their progress, and provide the teacher with an alternative way of measuring performance.

A1 students arriving in a new school can be assessed in relation to areas such as the ability to 'give personal information', or 'ask and answer simple questions', but the descriptor makes it clear that teacher support is appropriate 'to help me say what I want' even if a student is a successful A1 user. As accuracy is not such an important part of the student's achievement at that level, teachers are provided with a way of not simply evaluating but also 'valuing' the students' achievements.

Focus on speaking skills

In many secondary schools the programme tends to focus on reading and writing skills, and makes more progress in these than in speaking and listening. When matching a standard classroom syllabus with the CEF, one has to 'hold back' progress in reading and writing in order to allow the speaking and listening areas to catch up. This emphasis on speaking and listening allows the student to become a much more effective language user, so the CEF has an advantageous backwash effect.

This will impact on secondary teaching, but only gradually, as one cannot automatically change methodology by creating a new syllabus, or revolutionize a whole cultural attitude to language teaching overnight. Interestingly, however, the linking of the CEF with external exams such as those from Cambridge ESOL and Trinity College London, with their focus on oral performance, provides teachers with a genuine reason for focusing on oral competences.

Using the CEF in the classroom—some challenges

As I work extremely closely with the self-assessment descriptors when planning new courses, it is inevitable that incompatibilities start to emerge. For example, strengths, such as the move away from grammar, can become weaknesses when planning a syllabus based on a strong grammar framework. I outline below some difficulties I have encountered, which are found in the detail rather than the bigger picture.

No measure of grammar-based progression

While I acknowledge that a strength of the CEF is the way in which it replaces grammar with function, situation, information exchange, interaction, competences, skills, and strategies, I also believe that in the secondary classroom there is an inextricable link between a 'traditional' grammar-led syllabus and the performance-led syllabus of the CEF. There are grammar-based concept areas that are not covered early enough, or at all, which could be included, e.g. 'talking about the future'. These omissions strangely contradict the principles of the authors of the CEF, who challenge language curricula that delay working with the concept of past, and ask:

> ... should learners follow a progression which leaves them unable, after two years study, to speak of past experience?
> (CEF 2001: 151)

This is puzzling because courses do usually deal with past experience over a two-year programme, but I am interested in this statement for another reason. I believe that the CEF would be easier to use if it described other concept areas such as 'speak about the future', in the same way that it refers to 'speak of past experience'. The future is in fact only indirectly referred to in the descriptor 'make arrangements to meet' (A2). As most teachers also knowingly cover the concept of the future it is a shame that it is absent from the descriptors.

Overall there is not a consistent approach to grammar, or reference to commonly accepted concept areas such as the future, in the CEF descriptors. In the self-assessment grids (see Reference Document 2 in the Reference documents section of this book) the general descriptors only speak of a learner's manipulation of grammar in terms of 'use simple phrases', 'connect phrases in a simple way', and 'describe in simple terms'. These general descriptors are not sufficiently linked to concept areas to provide a basis for a teaching programme.

When there is a descriptor such as 'describe past activities' (A2), 'short narratives about everyday things' (A2), or 'narrating' (B1), it makes my job as a syllabus designer aiming to link the CEF with a grammar strand much easier. I can plan to cover items such as the past simple, the past continuous and time markers (obviously this operation would be different for another European language), and am thus able to position these grammar items in the syllabus at A2 level, while delaying the goal of full scale 'narration' to B1.

Linking concept areas with the descriptors would allow curriculum designers to link grammar and performance more easily. Areas such as 'talking about what is happening at the moment', 'reporting', 'talking about processes', 'expressing intentions and plans', 'talking about recent activities and achievements', 'making comparisons', 'talking about obligation', etc. could all be part of the self-assessment lists.

This is not to say that the guidelines for using the CEF ignore the role of grammar in the language classroom. In fact, the authors ask Framework users to consider questions of how structures are taught in the classroom:

> Users of the Framework may wish to consider and where appropriate state:

> — which grammatical elements, categories, classes, structures, processes and relations are learners etc. will need/be equipped/required to handle (p. 114)
> — the basis on which grammatical elements, categories, classes, structures, processes and relations are selected and ordered (p. 152)
> — how their meaning is conveyed to the learners (p. 152)
> — the role of contrastive grammar in language teaching and learning (p. 152)
> — the relative importance attached to range, fluency and accuracy in relation to the grammatical construction of sentences (p. 152)
> — the extent to which learners are to be made aware of the grammar of a) the mother tongue b) the target language c) their contrastive relations (p. 152)
> — how grammatical structure is a) analysed, ordered and presented to learners, and b) mastered by them.
> (CEF 2001: 152–53)

Despite the fact that the CEF places responsibility for developing students' grammatical competence with the materials developer, it doesn't provide the same flexibility in relation to situational/functional areas—where performance is quite clearly linked to certain attainment levels. As a course designer, I would be more comfortable if there were more guidance in relation to basic grammar areas too, instead of having to 'uncover' the grammatical areas that are inherent in the Framework.

The fact that CEF does not 'deal with' grammar also causes problems when grammar is inadvertently implied through the wording of the descriptors. The appearance of 'next week' and 'last Friday' at A1 level is difficult to handle, as I assume that an A1 user is not proficient enough to use the past and future structures that accompany these time phrases.

In short, my work has led me to believe that the CEF designers' 'soft touch' over grammar, understandable though it is given the philosophy of the CEF, simply creates an unnecessary barrier for teachers and course designers working with it.

Not necessarily suited to school-based learners

The CEF self-assessment descriptors often reflect a reality that seems more closely linked to the world of work, business, travel and cultural exchange, or academic work. There is an emphasis on booking hotels, arranging travel or writing reports. It also reflects performance in relation to interlocutors who are assumed in many cases to be either native speakers or at a higher level of competency than the student, something that would be likely in the 'real world'.

Therefore for you to 'qualify' as A1 level, your interlocutor may have to help you to clarify your meaning. But in the classroom it is probable that your interlocutor will be the same level as you, and this is not really reflected in the CEF. There is a general tone to the CEF that doesn't sound like the world of the classroom, and this can, sadly, make the CEF seem irrelevant to classroom achievements. The tenor of competences is also quite adult, and often not suited to the achievements and interests of a teenage or young adult learner.

Julia Starr Keddle

Individual self-assessment descriptors are not exhaustive	I realize that the CEF does not insist that anyone use its individual descriptors; in fact the authors help teachers to understand how they can adapt the CEF to their own reality. However, the fact is that most teachers and materials designers do not have time to design a CEF programme from scratch. Indeed, in Italy, there is a general unwritten agreement to use the self-assessment descriptors as a basic syllabus. Consequently, the quality of the self-assessment descriptors is of great significance, and any shortcomings have an impact on curriculum design.

One area which causes difficulty is where a competence in one skill is not reflected in its 'complementary' competence in another skill at the same level. For example, in A1, Listening: 'I can understand simple directions how to get from X to Y' is not matched with a similar descriptor in Spoken Interaction; instead this appears in the descriptors of A2 Spoken Interaction.

There is no doubt that being able to understand directions is a more basic competence than being able to give directions, but in the real world I do not believe that these two competences would be separated out, especially as you need to be able to ask for directions orally in order to be given them.

Of course, a descriptor for oral production of directions at A1 would need to contain 'if the speaker takes the trouble'. But from my own experience of 'survival' learning, I am able to give basic directions, e.g. 'go left' 'go right', once I am able to ask for and understand directions. In fact, communicatively speaking, you usually repeat instructions back to your interlocutor, e.g. 'left, then right'.

Some functional areas are not covered

The spoken interaction area of self-assessment statements links quite closely to a classic 'scope and sequence' description of functional/situational objectives. In A2 we find 'I can order something to eat and drink', 'I can ask for and give directions', 'I can make and respond to invitations'. In an equivalent level language course these objectives would be present, but there would be other functional areas covered, for example, accepting and refusing offers, talking about ability, giving advice, etc. In planning a syllabus, therefore, I have to reconcile the CEF statements with areas that seem equally appropriate for the level, but which are not specified.

Although Framework practitioners can add their own descriptors to the lists, the average teacher is neither aware of this, nor inclined to do the work needed, especially as the CEF gives the impression of being exhaustive in relation to functional areas. Teachers also expect a syllabus claiming to 'match' the CEF to reflect the official lists, and can be disorientated or disappointed when they are told that other areas have been added which are equally valid.

In addition there is an 'official' place where teachers find these descriptors being used, and that is the European Language Portfolio. It is entirely natural that students and teachers should expect their CEF-linked materials to be reflected in these lists. Instead, most coursebook-assessment checklists require students to tick off other descriptors that have been covered in the course, but which are not present on the lists.

To sum up, if the CEF functional descriptors were more comprehensive, and reflected the standard functional labelling used in the language classroom, they would be easier for teachers to understand and to use.

The CEF is not fully understood

There is no doubt that a lot of teachers are still not very aware of CEF, and are not trained to use it, which makes my work with it very sensitive. Some teachers confuse CEF with the Language Portfolio, or even see the CEF as a sort of European conspiracy to interfere with their teaching. Any work based on harmonizing their existing syllabus with CEF has to be shown to be advantageous, aimed at improving student performance, and simplifying teacher's work. In a way, that is why I am both an enthusiast of the CEF and a hard critic, as I have to proselytize it in my work and show teachers its benefits.

Conclusion

The CEF self-assessment checklists can look very daunting to students, especially to younger teenagers, and even to teachers. I feel that the way to approach this is to give the students ownership of the lists as soon as possible through Language Portfolio work. Students must feel that what they are doing in the classroom corresponds with the boxes they tick in their portfolio, and that the whole way of describing their performance makes sense. If this link is not clear then they will become demotivated, and in fact the descriptors will become counterproductive.

In my work I am trying to create an interface between the CEF and the classroom. I am committed to using the CEF as a tool to re-evaluate the standard syllabus strands, and create a syllabus that genuinely links the CEF with tried and tested expectations. It is a challenging task, but it is aided by the fact that both the CEF and the standard teaching programme for a secondary school course are the result of years of experience and knowledge. Both starting points are valid, but they have to work together in order to create something that brings language alive in the classroom, improves student performance, and makes life easier for the teacher. Despite some weaknesses, the CEF provides a broad, well-thought-out description of language competences, and is a challenging, thought-provoking tool for language teachers.

References
Coe, N., R. Rycroft, and **P. Ernest.** 1983. *Writing Skills.* Cambridge: Cambridge University Press.

The author

Julia Keddle has been involved in ELT for over 20 years. She taught in Italy for 10 years and in the UK at the Bell School. She is a teacher trainer and has worked for NILE. She worked in ELT publishing at Oxford University Press for 10 years, but is now a freelance writer, materials developer, and teacher trainer. She is the author of numerous test books and resource materials, and is co-author of Step Ahead Portfolio (ELI). She is currently working on ELT video projects, and is writing and developing courses based on the CEF.

Work in progress: a CEF/functional/grammar syllabus for a module from level 1 of a secondary school course.

A1 Module Talking about the past

Grammar	CEF areas to cover	Other functions
past simple verb *be*	*Listening:* understand simple conversation; understand basic personal information, family, shopping, local area, employment; identify main points of TV news items reporting events accidents, etc.	agreeing and disagreeing
past time expressions, e.g. *last night*		talking about the past
past simple: regular verbs /irregular verbs		talking about ability in the past
agreeing and disagreeing, e.g. *So do/did I. Neither do/did I.*		talking about obligation
		asking for and giving advice
subject/object questions	*Reading:* simple user's instructions; short narratives.	
could/was/were able to/managed to		
	Spoken interaction: say what I like and dislike; make and accept apologies; ask how people are and react to news.	
I'm keen on/I can't stand		
sequencers: *then/next* connectors: *and/but/or* obligation: modal verb *should*		
Why don't you?/You'd better	*Spoken production:* describe past events e.g. the past weekend; give short basic description of events; describe hobbies and interests.	
	Strategies: indicate I am following.	
	Language quality: link groups of words; use some simple structures correctly; cope with everyday situations; make myself understood with memorized phrases.	
	Writing: describe an event in simple sentences, e.g. party, accident; indicate chronological order.	

A plan for a unit that develops A2 CEF competencies, using the syllabus in Appendix 1.

Aims
- narrating
- interacting with someone narrating, helping by responding appropriately
- understanding a story.

CEF A2 Self-assessment descriptors

Spoken production: I can describe past activities and personal experiences (e.g. last weekend, my last holiday).

Strategies: I can indicate when I am following.

Language Quality: I can make myself understood using memorized phrases and single expressions; I can link groups of words with simple connectors (*and, but, because*).

Writing: I can use the most important connecting words used to indicate the chronological order of events (*first, then after, later*).

Main language points

Extension of use of past simple, connectors, sequencers

Conversation gambits, e.g. *Guess what happened next? You'll never believe it! And then what happened? Really? Did you? That's terrible/amazing* etc.

Main tasks
- Presentation of a picture story: comprehension and simple retelling.
- Listening to an anecdote: focus on comprehension and identifying exponents.
- Speaking: Information-gap picture story for students to narrate in groups/pairs.
- Extension: preparation of own real life story/anecdote.
- Speaking: Personalized story-telling in pairs.
- Writing: of own story using connecting words.

The CEF in pre- and in-service teacher education

Hanna Komorowska

Overview

This chapter examines the reception of the Common European Framework among teachers and teacher trainees in Poland, identifies difficulties connected with introducing the text of the document, and outlines possibilities of working with the CEF in pre- and in-service teacher education. Ideas presented here were developed during my experience as a teacher trainer and as the Polish delegate for the Modern Languages Project Group of the Council of Europe. Conclusions come from a qualitative action research project conducted at three teacher training institutions.

The social and educational context

The choice of the issues to be introduced into teacher education, and of the ways of working with the CEF, were to a large extent determined by the situation in post-transformation Poland. That is why a few comments on the national context might help to clarify the background to the project.

Poland in the mid-1990s

In the mid-1990s huge interest in the work on the CEF could be seen in Poland. Conference organizers wanted to include presentations of this work. Teachers' organizations and professional journals were interested in the outcomes, and individual teachers wanted to know as much as possible about what was going on in Strasbourg.

The reasons for this immense interest were twofold. Firstly, after many years of having been cut off from European influences, Poland opened up to the Western world. Teachers now wanted to know what new ideas might help them design their own curricula, as these were no longer centralized, to choose course books that could at last be freely selected, and to make decisions about language education in newly established non-state primary and secondary schools. Teacher trainers working in the new system of training foreign language teachers which was established in 1990, and running new in-service courses, did not want to miss out on any professional novelty, especially since a market for paid educational services had emerged. Secondly, the profession felt the need to find 'the right way ahead', as the tradition of single right answers was definitely at work. There was a need for models to be followed and ideas to be reflected on. In this context, promoting the CEF ideas in pre- and in-service teacher education seemed not only necessary but also relatively easy.

A change in attitude

The situation changed towards the end of the 1990s. The work on the Framework took a long time, and documentation arriving in the meantime was difficult to understand. It became more or less obvious that no clear-cut recommendations or evaluative judgements were to be expected. Questions were no longer asked. The work to develop the CEF was almost forgotten by teachers except for those who participated in Graz seminars and the Council of Europe networks. Only publishers and teacher trainers worked on the promotion of the CEF ideas, though this was getting increasingly more difficult due to the lack of motivation on the part of the audience.

A background role

Although rank and file teachers paid little attention to the CEF at that time, it had a great impact on the Polish education system. This was because of its influence on syllabus and materials design related to the reform of the school system and teacher education, both of which were being implemented in Poland at that time. However, many teachers remained unaware of the role of the CEF as a driving force behind these changes (Komorowska 2002).

A new wave of interest in the document itself could be seen in 2002, i.e. after the publication of the CEF by Cambridge University Press. Motivation increased with the development of new European Union projects in the field of language testing which were based on the descriptors used in the CEF document. (See the chapter by Ari Huhta and Neus Figueras in this collection.) Teachers, school principals, educational managers, and members of the regional self-government bodies who were now engaged, or hoping to get involved in, e.g. Leonardo da Vinci projects, were now desperate to get acquainted with the CEF. Strong pressure on the Polish government was then exerted to find resources to have the document translated into Polish. At the time of writing (November 2003), this is due to be published very shortly.

Introducing the CEF into teacher education

When the first draft of the Common European Framework was published in its mimeographed form in Strasbourg in late 1996, the interest in the work of the Council of Europe in general, and in the work on the CEF in particular, was at its peak in Poland. That is why it seemed only natural to get teacher trainees acquainted with it as soon as possible. After a short try-out in 1997, I started working with the original text in pre-and in-service teacher training during the academic year 1998–9. The exercise proved much more difficult than expected, and for this reason grew into a three-cycle action research project, based in each cycle on a sample of three different groups of students studying through the medium of English.

Groups

The first group was made up of students at the first and second year of the three-year course at Warsaw University Teacher Training College, and at the University of Bialystok.[1] They had minimum academic background and no real teaching experience, which was to come in the third year of their BA track. I worked with these students during a two-semester interactive lecture course covering broad topics related to the psychological and pedagogical foundations of foreign language teaching. Groups were often combined to form audiences of 30 to 45 students.

The second group consisted of students following the five-year MA track at the Institute of English who, in their third and fourth years, decided to take courses in foreign language teaching methodology in order to obtain teaching qualifications, which were not automatically carried by their MA diploma. Their academic background was considerable, but very few of them had teaching experience other than private one-to-one lessons. With these students I worked on one-semester courses entitled 'Syllabus design', 'Classroom interaction', and 'Second Language Acquisition and Language Pedagogy', using the CEF as a contribution to these courses.

The third group was a group of active teachers, BA or BEd holders, in the second year of a three-year extramural track offered as a follow-up MA for graduates from three-year teacher training colleges. Their academic background was similar to that of the students in group 2, and their teaching experience was considerable. They discussed the CEF during an MA seminar while working on their MA dissertations on various topics related to English language teaching methodology.

First cycle: introducing the CEF as a document

Initially, that is during the first year of my work with the CEF, all the groups were expected to read and discuss parts which in the Cambridge University Press, 2001 edition of the document form Chapters 1, 2, 4, 5, 6, and 8. We also worked through some of the descriptors.

The basic difference in the way of introducing the CEF to all the groups consisted in the form of the work with the text: group 1, i.e. the youngest and the least experienced students had a brief mini-lecture introduction, and then received excerpts from the CEF on handouts, reading them in class and discussing them immediately afterwards with a follow-up lecture round-up; the other two groups read chapters at home and discussed them in class. There was also some difference in the amount of text read and discussed: group 1 read and discussed only relatively small excerpts; group 2 read and discussed large excerpts or whole chapters (usually three or four chapters); and group 3, that is the group of active teachers, read and discussed all the chapters listed above.

Text difficulty

All the three groups found the text extremely difficult to read and understand, though group 3, i.e. active teachers, BA holders working towards their MA in Philology, found the CEF much less difficult to go through than the other students. However, being much more assertive and aware of their needs, they voiced a lot more complaints. These were mainly related to the complexity of the text. Students criticized both the length of the document and its structure, pointing to overlaps, especially in chapters related to language use, language learning, and language teaching; they also complained about never-ending typologies and lists.

Similar complaints, though not so clearly presented, came from students of the five-year MA track. These students, however, mainly stressed the amount of reading, which is understandable in relation to the fact that they had to cope with the CEF within a one- semester course originally devoted to other problems, so the CEF was only part of their background reading.

First year students at the Teacher Training College were the most cautious of all the three groups in voicing their problems. Perhaps a more general tendency was at work here: secondary school graduates, freshly installed at the university and not yet well acquainted with academic texts, usually find it difficult to identify sources of their problems, and tend to blame themselves rather than the reading material.

Varying interests of students

Students from the Teacher Training College, though they could be expected to show interest in the practical aspects of teaching languages, were not at all enthusiastic about them, probably due to their lack of teaching experience. Consequently they felt no need to deal with the educational context in roles other than those of the learners. They were, however, very interested in ways of working on an international document, and especially in the criteria to be met by the CEF. (See CEF Chapter 1.6.)

Students from the academic track were mainly interested in general competences, learner variables, and some issues relating to language learning and teaching, e.g. the choice of learning strategies and strategy training.

Professionally active teachers from the extra-mural track, on the other hand were interested in curriculum scenarios and—first of all—in assessment and descriptors.

Second cycle: introducing ideas from the CEF

The combination of these two factors, that is of varying text difficulty for particular groups and varying interests displayed by them, called for a new approach. Although clear differences could be seen in the way the CEF was introduced to the three groups in the first cycle, more needed to be done in this area. Therefore, a new approach was adopted in the second cycle, i.e. in the academic years 1999–2000 and 2000–1.

Working with selected issues

As the youngest and least experienced students of the Teacher Training College found the original text excessively difficult, but were very interested in the way it had been prepared, a move to a strictly lecture-type presentation of the CEF, supported by transparencies shown on an OHP seemed to be a better solution. Presentation followed by discussion was spread over three meetings, and concentrated on the following issues:

- reasons for the decision to start work on the preparation of the CEF in Strasbourg
- criteria to be met by the final version of the document
- activities, domains, topics, and tasks.

Over four successive semesters, two ways of integrating these presentations into the overall curriculum of the training programme were tried out.

The first way was to offer the sessions as early as possible, i.e. at the beginning of the second semester of the first year of studies, in order to target the moment when students are not yet used to any specific way of using terminology. The second way was to offer the CEF sessions as late as possible, i.e. at the end of the first semester of the second year of their studies, when they are already well acquainted with the terminology, are well aware of differences in the use of terms, and are able to compare them.

Students of the five-year MA track taking one-semester courses were now given only a selection of chapters, sometimes even no more than a section within a chapter, this time concentrating on activities, domains, topics, and tasks in relation to some selected learner characteristics, always in relation to the type of their course.

Finally, active teachers followed the course in the way most similar to what the former group of the same track had been doing during the previous year. The only changes introduced here were to encourage comparisons between the CEF and other descriptions of the teaching and learning process, to emphasize the issues of partial competences and curriculum scenarios, and to encourage students to reflect on practical applications of these ideas in their schools.

Effect of these changes

The lecture-cum-discussion type of presentation for first and second year students of the Teacher Training College elicited much more interest on the part of the students, who asked a lot of questions and made a lot of interesting comments, especially about the learner's role, which demonstrated that they understood a lot more of the CEF as a result of the simplified presentation. It was then easy to see that the high degree of difficulty encountered by students of the same institution in the previous year was connected with the language and style of the text, and not with the complexity of ideas. The lecture, however, had the obvious disadvantage of distancing students , if not discouraging them, from reading the text on their own—a natural consequence of their relying on class presentation.

All in all, though, it proved to be a happier solution than reading excerpts and discussing them, which had been the format introduced previously. It also became clear that the second option of introducing the CEF sessions as late as possible, i.e. in the second year of their studies at the Teacher Training College, seemed to function far better.

Students of the five-year MA track taking one-semester methodology courses, seemed, paradoxically, to benefit more from reading less, as they seemed to concentrate better, understand much more, and were, therefore, able to relate the CEF much more directly to the main topic of their course. Unexpected effects, however, appeared as well. Now that students were reading less, and could concentrate on the quality of the text, they started voicing complaints about terminology and text difficulty of the same sort that active teachers in the follow-up MA track had been voicing from the very beginning. The only part they found quite clear was the descriptors.

New groups of active teachers continued voicing the same type of complaints, and again pointed to descriptors as the only clear part of the document. They found the issue of partial competences very difficult to understand (perhaps due to the all or nothing approaches typical of their own past education) and could not find ways to apply this concept in their own teaching practice. Curriculum scenarios, on the other hand, seemed interesting as a topic for almost everybody, and created no problems because of the relative clarity of the CEF presentation of the area.

Problem issues

In the second cycle, the following issues caused real problems:

- terminology

  Students were appalled to find that most of the terms and typologies they had learnt so far were replaced by new terms. What they knew as 'components of the communicative ability' (or competence), e.g. linguistic, communicative, strategic, sociocultural, etc. had to disappear, as the term 'components of the communicative competence' now covered only three areas (linguistic, sociolinguistic, pragmatic). They got confused as the term 'competence' was also used for the four types of 'savoir', not to mention, e.g. phonological competence. What they knew as 'skills' now became 'activities', although they were used to the term 'communicative activities' in the meaning of class tasks, etc.

- lack of practical guidelines as to the choices to be made

  Practising teachers felt they were left alone when it came to any kind of decision making, as lists of options were not followed by recommendations. For school teachers difficulties were related to curriculum scenarios, and to the selection of learning strategies to be supported or trained, while for language school teachers difficulties were more often related to the selection of competences to be developed, domains, and teaching methods.

  Terminology made it worse as, not understanding why the traditional distinction of language elements and skills had to go, they now had problems in applying the CEF categories to course book evaluation and selection.

- non-evaluative character of the CEF

  Neither teacher trainees nor practising teachers could easily accept the fact that the same value was ascribed to very different approaches. For example, the communicative and the grammar-translation methods were listed in the CEF as examples within the same typology. For example, they were afraid that this made it possible for the school principal to impose the grammar-translation method on them, pointing to the Framework as a legitimate excuse.

Issues of interest

Young trainees continued to show a great interest in the way international bodies work and were therefore, more interested in the ideas from Chapter 1, 'The Common European Framework in its political and educational context', and Chapter 2, 'Approach adopted'.

Hanna Komorowska

Students working towards teacher qualification during their five-year MA studies were more interested in aspects of language acquisition, learning and use, as well as in academic ways of presenting those issues, and for that reason they found Chapter 4 'Language use and the language user/learner' and Chapter 5, 'The user/learner's competences', most interesting.

Practising teachers in in-service education were attracted by issues connected with decision-making at the school and at the classroom level. Ideas from Chapter 6, 'Language learning and teaching', and Chapter 8, 'Linguistic diversification and the curriculum', were the most valuable for them.

Some shared interests could also be noticed. Chapter 3, 'Common reference levels', presenting descriptors and 'can do' statements was the hit of the course for everybody, though all the students were disappointed to find out that 90 per cent of their learners are, and will remain, around the B1 level. Descriptors included in Chapter 5, 'The user/learner's competences', proved far less interesting for most of the students.

Third cycle: applying ideas from the CEF Integrating the CEF into individual work and alternative assessment

The third cycle was initiated in the academic year 2001–2. This, however, took place in a slightly changed situation as the students' awareness of the CEF had changed as a result both of the publication of the document by Cambridge University Press, and the introduction of Common Reference Levels into placement procedures and descriptions of exit competences at various institutions, including Warsaw University School of Foreign Languages.

Integration

This time, the procedures adopted in the former cycle seemed quite satisfactory, except for the one selected for the youngest students. As far as this group was concerned, more integration of the CEF categories with the rest of the course was needed. It seemed that for all the groups changes should now be extended to cover not only what was going on in class, but also the individual work of students, and the way they were assessed.

In the previous cycles the youngest students from the Teacher Training College seemed eager to take the learner's point of view rather than the teacher's perspective. This was a good starting point for the change of a test-based credit into a reflection-based assignment in the form of a self-profile. The analysis undertaken by each student was to cover his/her educational background and the history of his/her English language education based on categories introduced in the Common European Framework.

Students were asked to prepare their personal learning histories in the form of a portfolio, adding comments on aspects introduced at particular sessions, though some of them decided to prepare their histories at the very end of the course. Their grade depended on the number of categories included and on the depth (but not length) of their analysis, as well as on their decision whether or not to include an extra history related to a foreign language other than English.

Students of the five-year MA track taking one-semester methodology courses, who were expected to write a term paper on one of 12 selected topics related to their course, received an extra task of relating their term paper to a relevant category of the CEF. If more than one category applied, they had a choice of including them all, or concentrating on one of them only.

Active teachers from extra-mural BA tracks, whose credit had formerly been based on an end-of-semester test, had seemed in the second cycle to be happier taking the teacher's rather than the learner's perspective. That is why their test has been changed—much along the lines of the change in the youngest students' assessment—into an analysis of their own teaching situation in a selected class according to categories listed in the CEF. They were also asked to prepare their analysis in the form of a portfolio, introducing new portions of comments on aspects as they were introduced in sessions. Their grade—like that of the youngest students— depended on the number of categories included, and on the depth of their analysis. Top marks were given to those who included an extra component with a case study of one of their learners, and teaching recommendations based on this analysis.

As the reaction of students in all the three groups was quite positive, this form of work aiming at the integration of the CEF with the teaching content of pre-and in-service teacher education is now being continued. Further changes, if needed, will be introduced when the Polish translation of the CEF makes its way into the bookshops.

Conclusions

Experience so far has clearly demonstrated that:
- The Common European Framework is not particularly user-friendly when it comes to the individual work of the trainee with the text. Introducing the document is, therefore, greatly facilitated if the teacher-trainer gives a presentation of a mini-lecture type preceding discussion, as this helps to clarify ideas and to explain terminology used differently from the way it is used in most writing about foreign language teaching.
- Individual work can be safely introduced later and combined with students' project work and assessment.
- Trainees in pre-service teacher education seem to benefit from the CEF ideas if they look at them from the learner's perspective, possibly reflecting on the course of their present and past language education, analysing outcomes of their learning, and reflecting on how their learning was affected by:
  — teachers' roles
  — methods and techniques used by teachers
  — assessment functioning in their schools
  — their own learning strategies.
- Teachers in in-service teacher training seem to benefit more when they take the teacher's perspective, and use the CEF categories to do the following:
  a to work on a profile of a selected learner looking at his/her strengths and weaknesses, in particular at:
  — competences

Hanna Komorowska

— language activities
— learning strategies
— levels attained
and then present as well as justify decisions to be taken.
  b to work on a case study of a group of learners with the view to modelling future decisions related to:
— the curriculum scenario to be implemented
— levels to be attained
— activities to be emphasized
— tasks to be introduced
— learning strategies to be trained and/or supported.

■ Students in academic tracks who decide to work towards their teaching qualification in parallel to their university diploma seem to benefit, both during class discussions and in their term papers, from attempts to apply CEF categories to the content of the academic courses they actually take.

Difficulties are, however, to be expected connected with the overlap of issues discussed in particular chapters of the Framework, and with terminology which tends to confuse readers. When difficulties prove insurmountable, the teacher trainer can always turn to levels and descriptors which—through 'can do' statements—unfailingly show the value of the CEF both for those who take the learner's perspective and those who take that of the teacher. Most probably that is why this has become the best known part of the document so far.

Notes

1 In Poland there are a number of pre-service and in-service routes which teachers may follow:

  a three-year philological + teacher education university programmes that offer a BA plus a teaching qualification, called university colleges (group 1 in my action research).
  b three-year philological programmes that offer a philological BA with no teaching qualification.
  c three-year postsecondary schools under the supervision of universities which offer a final certificate with a teaching qualification but no BA, called Local Educational Authorities colleges.
  d five-year philological MA programmes with an optional teacher education component which leads to a qualification in parallel to the MA diploma (group 2 in my action research).
  e follow-up MA programmes for practising teachers, graduates from three-year BA tracks (group 3 of my action research).

References

Council of Europe. 1996. *Common European Framework for Language Teaching and Learning.* 1996. Strasbourg: The Council of Europe.
Council of Europe. 2001. *Common European Framework of Reference for Languages: Learning, Teaching, Assessment.* Cambridge: Cambridge University Press.
Also available for download from http://www.coe.int/T/E/Cultural_Co-operation/education/Languages/Language_Policy/Common_Framework_of_Reference/1cadre.asp#TopOfPage.
Council of Europe. 2003. *Europejski system opisu kształcenia językowego: uczenie się, nauczania, ocenianie.* Warszawa: Wydawnictwa CODN.
Komorowska, H. 2002. 'The Common European Framework in Poland' in *Common European Framework of Reference for Languages: Learning, Teaching, Assessment. Case Studies.* Strasbourg: The Council of Europe Publications.

The author

Hanna Komorowska is Professor of Applied Linguistics at the Institute of English, Warsaw University, and the head of the expert committee for foreign language teaching and teacher education reform in post-transformation Poland. She is the Polish delegate to the Modern Languages Section of the Council of Europe, and a consultant for the European Language Portfolio at the Polish Ministry of Education. She has published widely in the field of EFL methodology, language testing, and teacher education.

Hanna Komorowska

Using the CEF to promote language learning through diagnostic testing

Ari Huhta and Neus Figueras

Overview

DIALANG is a diagnostic language assessment system available on the Internet in 14 European languages. It gives learners a variety of feedback on the strong and weak points in their proficiency, and advice for further learning. It also aims at raising the users' awareness of various aspects of language learning and proficiency. This chapter describes how the system is related to the Common European Framework, and how it aims to support language learning and teaching in Europe.

What is DIALANG?

DIALANG is a diagnostic language assessment system in 14 European languages available on the Internet free of charge. It was developed with the financial support of the SOCRATES Programme of the European Union (LINGUA Action D) and DIALANG project partners. See the DIALANG web site for details of the project partners, and for access to the assessment system.

In the DIALANG system 'diagnosis' is understood in very general terms. The test gives language learners feedback about the strengths and weaknesses in their proficiency, rather than providing a 'clinical' diagnosis of, for example, learning problems. Diagnosis given by DIALANG is not directly related to specific language courses or curricula (cf. Spolsky 1992), rather, it builds on the specifications of language proficiency presented in the Common European Framework (CEF).

Aims

The project was designed to help to disseminate the philosophy and the contents of the CEF to users of different kinds: learners, teachers, institutions, ministries, etc. The first draft of the CEF (1996) was immediately perceived as an important document, but also as a document which was complex and difficult to use. DIALANG aimed to show that the CEF could be used to create a transparent, European framework for language assessment purposes.

The DIALANG partnership set out to develop a system which, like the CEF, would be transparent, open, and innovative, and also non-threatening and acceptable in different contexts by different stakeholders. Diagnostic testing seemed to best integrate those purposes: it lent itself to the incorporation of the main features of the CEF, and it was low stakes, i.e. involving no crucial decisions about the learners, unlike testing for certification purposes. Furthermore, it offered the chance to make innovative use of Information Technology in presenting more to the learners than just computerized versions of paper-and-pencil tests.

Using the CEF

This chapter presents an overview of how the CEF (the 1996 version) is applied in DIALANG. Further details are given in Appendix C of the CEF 2001, and Huhta, Luoma, Oscarson, Sajavaara, Takala, and Teasdale 2002.

For the benefit of the users of the CEF, the chapter contains not only information about the way the CEF was used but also discussion of where the CEF was found to be lacking in content in the development of our assessment system. We start at the planning stages of the system and then describe the development of the self-assessment and feedback sections.

DIALANG framework and specifications

DIALANG's Assessment Framework (DAF) sets out the theoretical framework for the system, and the DIALANG Assessment Specifications (DAS) describe how the framework is translated into concrete tasks. The Assessment Framework is directly based on the CEF, whereas the Assessment Specifications make use of the CEF, but derive a lot of their content from other sources.

The Assessment Framework summarizes the relevant content of the CEF, including the six-point reference scale, communicative tasks and purposes, themes and specific notions, activities, texts, and functions. For the benefit of the DIALANG item writers, the DAF also presents very detailed lists of the above CEF categories, supplemented with material extracted from the Council of Europe Waystage, Threshold, and Vantage-level publications.

As noted above, the DIALANG Assessment Specifications are only partially based on the Common Framework because item writing guidelines require specific information that is simply not available in the CEF.

The CEF was very useful for defining language use situations, functions, and topics to be tested, and DIALANG item writers were provided with checklists to ensure that their items covered these categories thoroughly enough. However, the CEF could not be used to specify the item writing process nor the actual test tasks; instead, the project made use of relevant language testing literature (e.g. Alderson et al. 1995).

Limitations of the CEF

For task difficulty and text types, the project had to look elsewhere. The CEF discusses some dimensions of difficulty, such as text characteristics, and types of response, but those only account for part of task difficulty. The CEF also lists different sources for written and spoken texts (books, magazines, announcements, etc.) but to specify the texts in more detail the project referred to the typology of textual organization proposed by Werlich (1988).

The specification of the areas or subskills that DIALANG tests were to cover was not based on the CEF either. Thus, the decision, for example, to

Ari Huhta and Neus Figueras

define reading and listening in terms of 'understanding main ideas', 'understanding specific details', and 'making inferences' came from other sources (see the next section for an example of feedback on subskills).

And finally, the CEF had only very little material that could be directly used as the basis of vocabulary and grammar tests. It was thus necessary for the project to design its own, language-specific specifications for vocabulary and structures.

<table>
<tr><td>Contribution of the CEF</td><td>However, the CEF was crucial in the development of two of the most significant components of the DIALANG assessment system, self-assessment and feedback.</td></tr>
</table>

Self-assessment

First of all, the decision to use the CEF provided the project with an excellent opportunity to develop self-assessment instruments, since the work of North (1995) included a considerable number of descriptive statements of language proficiency in English which had been trialled, validated, and calibrated. DIALANG selected a number of statements from the CEF, and adapted them for self-assessment purposes, which involved some simplification to clarify them for learners.

Here is an example of the way in which an A2 level (Waystage) statement was simplified:

CEF: Can understand short, simple texts on familiar matters of a concrete type which consist of high frequency everyday language or job-related language.

This text was split into two simpler statements:

DIALANG: I can understand short, simple texts written in common everyday language.
DIALANG: I can understand short simple texts related to my job.

Also, a small number of new statements had to be created, (e.g. for writing) because the statements in the CEF (1996) did not fully cover all aspects and levels of proficiency.

The modified English language statements were translated into the 13 other languages (see www.dialang.org, and Huhta et al. 2002 for details on the development process). The translated statements were pilot-tested together with the test items, analysed statistically, and turned into self-assessment instruments, which the user can take before taking a language test. Each of the self-assessment instruments contains 18 statements.

Feedback

In terms of the development of DIALANG feedback, the input from the CEF was most extensive in the sections that contain descriptions of proficiency levels, i.e. in the test result, self-assessment feedback, and the more elaborated level descriptions. However, it is also present in the pedagogical philosophy and intentions behind all feedback.

DIALANG aims to provide its users with information to enable them to analyse their strengths and weaknesses, and to plan further language learning. Therefore it presents them a range of different types of feedback:

1 They get a test result as a level in the skill they selected.

2 They are informed if the self-assessment they completed before the test differed from the test result, and they can view explanations of possible reasons for a mismatch.

3 They can review all the test tasks they have taken.

4 They have access to more detailed descriptions of their level of proficiency, and to advice on how to improve their skills.

The influence of the CEF on all these areas is considerable:

1 The DIALANG test result is reported on the Council of Europe six-level scale. The names of the levels are exactly the same as in the CEF, i.e. A1, A2, B1, B2, C1, and C2. The descriptions of the level are also very directly derived from the CEF scale descriptions (see Appendix C in the CEF 2001).

2 Feedback involving the comparison of the learner's self-assessment and test result is also based on the CEF scales. The way in which the self-assessment instrument itself derives its content from the descriptors of proficiency in the CEF was set out above. However, the whole idea of comparing self-assessment and test performance would not be possible without the CEF scale, and the linking of both the self-assessment statements and the test tasks to this common scale.

3 More detailed descriptions of the six CEF levels are provided. For an example see below under 'Advisory feedback' (Figure 6 on p. 11; see also Appendix C in the CEF 2001). These descriptions elaborate on the nature of comprehension or production typical of each level.

4 In addition to the detailed descriptions, this part of the feedback contains advice to the users on how to improve their skills. Some content for the advice comes from the sections in the CEF on language learning and teaching methodology, study skills, and strategies.

5 Finally, the explanations for possible reasons for a mismatch between self-assessment and test result are inspired by the CEF, which encourages the development of awareness in language learners about different aspects of their learning. The explanations aim at increasing the learners' awareness of their language proficiency, including their own view of its level and adequacy for different purposes, and of a number of factors that relate to language use and learning. However, most of the concrete content in that section comes from other sources other than the CEF.

Self-assessment and feedback as learner training instruments

The concept of learner training is not new. It goes back to the Chinese saying, 'Give a man a fish, and you feed him for a day. Teach a man to fish, and you feed him for life.'

Ari Huhta and Neus Figueras

Specific literature on learner training goes back to the 1970s. Publications in the area have treated such important topics as being a good language learner (Rubin 1975; Naiman et al. 1978), autonomous learning (Holec 1980) and learning strategies—how they might be taught and learnt (Oxford 1990; O'Malley and Chamot 1990; Ellis and Sinclair 1989). Learner awareness (van Lier 1996) and self-assessment (Oscarson 1997; Kohonen 1999) have also received attention. However, on the whole, given its importance, this work has not received as much attention in terms of its underlying theoretical principles as it deserved. Thanks to the CEF, the situation has now somewhat changed in that this brings together, in a principled way, many of the topics discussed in the literature quoted above.

DIALANG set out to facilitate independent learning and to raise learners' awareness about how languages are learnt through access to varied, on-line materials and fully developed self-assessment and feedback components. This implied looking at diagnostic testing from a new perspective, going beyond what in the introductory paragraph was labelled as 'clinical' diagnosis to a detailed focus on students' own judgements about their language ability, and on test performances.

Self-assessment and self-awareness

A key feature of DIALANG is the aim to increase the learners' self-awareness. This is nowadays considered to be an essential element in language learning (O'Malley and Chamot 1990; Oxford 1990; Oscarson 1997).

How does self-assessment in DIALANG increase the users' awareness? There are three ways in which it does this:

1 The very act of self-assessment is a means of stimulating the learners to reflect on their strengths and weaknesses—they have to decide whether they can do the tasks described in the self-assessment statements presented by the system (Figure 1 below). Self-assessment in DIALANG is not only a testing instrument but it should also be considered as a learning tool.

2 The feedback on the match, or mismatch, between self-assessment and the test result informs them about the relationship between the two.

3 By studying the potential reasons for a mismatch the learners can further reflect on their abilities, views of language proficiency, of language tests, and other factors that potentially relate to language learning (Figure 4 below).

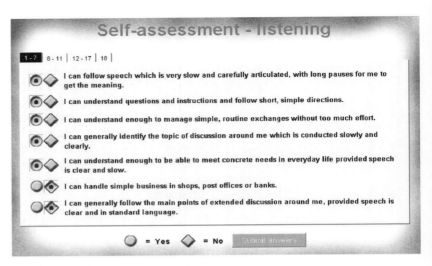

FIGURE 1 Examples of DIALANG self-assessment statements.

DIALANG and the European Language Portfolio

The DIALANG self-assessment component is even more relevant now than it was when the system was developed, as assessing oneself on the basis of CEF descriptors is an important part of the European Language Portfolio—ELP. (See www.coe.int, under Modern languages, and the chapter by Peter Lenz in this collection.)

DIALANG also shares the two main functions of the ELP: the reporting function and the pedagogical function. DIALANG self-assessment is helpful for users as they need to think of their language level in terms of the CEF descriptors. In the same way they have to report on what they can do and they cannot do in ELP. But self-assessment has also been reported (Oscarson 1990) to encourage autonomous learning, give learners control over their own learning, and enhance awareness of the learning process—all points appearing in the CEF.

Achieving the above is not easy or straightforward, either for learners or for those trying to help them. Self-assessment is not easy, and using the CEF descriptors may be too demanding for some users without any training or interest in self-assessment. It is expected that one of the beneficial effects of the widespread use of the ELP in primary and secondary levels will be to increase the familiarity of European learners with this approach to learning and assessment.

The feedback component

Feedback in DIALANG is also related to the principles behind the CEF and the ELP. Firstly, it is designed to have a pedagogical impact as the learner's test performance is reported in a way that aims to help them. Secondly, feedback is varied enough so that different users can benefit from it in different learning contexts. As feedback is perhaps the most innovative feature of DIALANG, it is worth presenting in some detail.

Once learners have completed an assessment cycle in DIALANG, which may have included immediate (right/wrong) feedback after each item whilst doing the test, they are presented with five types of feedback:

Ari Huhta and Neus Figueras

1 The level of proficiency as a CEF level

The learner's test result is expressed as a CEF level, accompanied with a description of what learners at that level can do (see Figure 2).

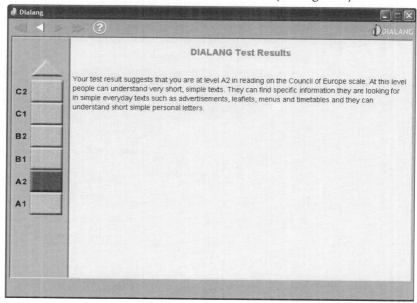

FIGURE 2   DIALANG test result screen for level A2 in reading.

2 Review of test tasks

Here the learners can review the tasks they answered during the test. The tasks presented are grouped according to right and wrong responses, and further divided into subskills to provide the learners with more information (see Figure 3). When learners click on an item tab, they can see their own answer and check the acceptable answers for that task.

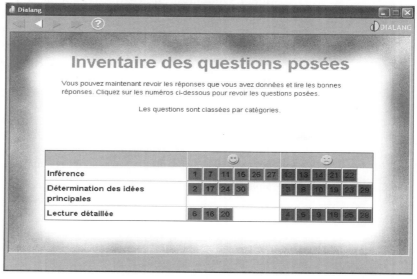

FIGURE 3   The main item review screen (a reading test with French as the language of instruction).

3 Match between self-assessment and test result

If the learners responded to the self-assessment statements, they can access information on whether their self-assessment matched their test result; the match is expressed in terms of the CEF levels. They can also access explanations about possible reasons for mismatch between self-assessment and test results, and they are encouraged to identify for themselves the reasons that may have applied in their case (see Figure 4).

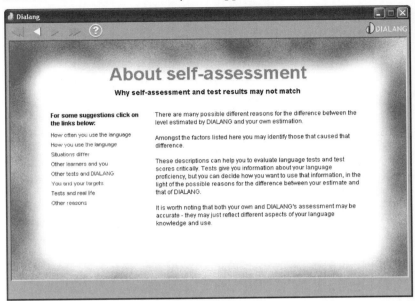

FIGURE 4 Introductory screen for possible reasons for a mismatch between self-assessment and test result.

An example of awareness-raising feedback that refers to the CEF is found under 'Other tests and DIALANG' (on the left in Figure 4) and is presented in Figure 5:

DIALANG and other international language tests

In some languages learners can take international language tests, that is, tests that are administered and recognised in many countries. As with some school-based or national tests, some of these international tests can give you a fairly good idea where you stand against an international yardstick such as the Council of Europe six-point scale. However, you need to study what the test producers say about the meaning of their grades: some may report their results by using descriptions of their grades that are similar to those used in the Council of Europe scale. To what extent do the two descriptions match or differ?

Note also that some international tests are specific to certain occupations or fields, which limits their comparability with DIALANG.

FIGURE 5 Example of awareness-raising information found in self-assessment feedback.

Ari Huhta and Neus Figueras

4 At the beginning of a DIALANG test session, the user can take an optional Vocabulary Size Placement Test. The users are reported a score (0–1,000), and a description of how to interpret the score, for example:

> People who score at this level typically have a good basic vocabulary, but may have difficulty handling material that is intended for native speakers.

5 Advisory feedback. In this section, the learner can access extra information on the level of proficiency assigned to him/her by the system, and on the two levels next to it (Figure 6). We have found that this enables some learners to see more clearly where they stand on the CEF scale. As described earlier, these descriptions are based on the material in the CEF. Advisory feedback also contains advice on how to progress to the following level (Figure 7).

	A1	A2	B1
What types of text I understand	Very short, simple texts, typically short, simple descriptions, especially if they contain pictures. Short, simple written instructions e.g. short simple postcards, simple notices.	Texts on familiar, concrete matters. Short, simple texts e.g. routine personal and business letters and faxes, most everyday signs and notices, Yellow Pages, advertisements.	Straightforward factual texts on subjects related to my field of interest. Everyday material, e.g. letters, brochures and short official documents. Straightforward newspaper articles on familiar subjects and descriptions of events. Clearly written argumentative texts. Personal letters expressing feelings and wishes. Clearly written, straightforward instructions for a piece of equipment.
What I understand	Familiar names, words, basic phrases.	Understand short simple texts. Find specific information in simple everyday material.	Understand straightforward factual language. Understand clearly written general argumentation (but not necessarily all details). Understand straightforward instructions. Find general information I need in everyday material. Locate specific information by searching one long or several different texts.
Conditions and limitations	Single phrase at a time, re-reading parts of text.	Restricted mainly to common everyday language and language related to my job.	Ability to identify main conclusions and follow argument restricted to straightforward texts.

FIGURE 6 Extended descriptions of the CEF levels. This shows some of the key differences between A2, the level below (A1) and the level above (B1).

The following suggestions may help you make progress towards B1:

— Increase the range and type of texts you actively try to read. You might like to look at newspapers and magazines in English and work at one or two of the more difficult articles which interest you, with a dictionary if necessary.
— Pay special attention to particular expressions, phrases, and words in English used for argumentation, description, and to express feelings and wishes.
— Try to understand the details of particular texts rather than making do with the main ideas. Keep a notebook where you write the expressions which you think are useful and worth remembering.
— Ensure that you read a lot in English. Although you can already understand a lot of what you read, you need to actively develop your reading skills by ensuring that you regularly read a lot, and that you occasionally read more difficult texts in some depth.

FIGURE 7 Advice on how to improve reading from level A2 towards B1, for a user who has taken a reading test of English.

To sum up, DIALANG feedback can be characterized as:

1 user-friendly and accessible: written for lay people; available in 14 languages

2 based on the Common Framework, and thus on an international, comparable and transparent yardstick (the main test result and self-assessment feedback in particular)

3 immediate and contextualized: given immediately after the test, or each task; related to tests, tasks, or self-assessment completed during the same session

4 varied: ranging from concrete test tasks to more abstract ideas about proficiency and learning

5 optional and modular: users can decide what feedback to read, and for how long.

Lessons learnt and the way forward

How do users appreciate DIALANG system and its feedback? Reactions suggest that learners, teachers, and institutions alike find it useful that DIALANG reports the test takers' results against the CEF levels, which are becoming an international yardstick (see www.dialang.org for more information).

The system allows comparisons of proficiency across different settings, and is useful, for example, for placement purposes. Furthermore, the descriptions of proficiency based on the CEF are felt to be much more informative than the mere numbers that many learners are used to getting from language tests. The very idea of thinking of proficiency in terms of levels also appears to be new in many educational contexts, and DIALANG provides a concrete instrument with which to familiarize oneself with the CEF, its levels, and its view of language in general.

First reactions to DIALANG have thus been very positive, and a number of uses for the system have been identified. However, using DIALANG to its full potential will take some time. But this should not come as a surprise. Henri Holec back in the 1980s insisted on the importance of

Ari Huhta and Neus Figueras

training students to become autonomous, and pointed out the difficulties of improving self-directed learning. Becoming autonomous is a long process of personal development and discovery. Furthermore, additional pedagogic support is often useful for learners using DIALANG—either face-to-face (by teacher) or based on specific materials, which may result in retaking DIALANG, and thus becoming more and more familiar with its structure and principles.

Having presented the system in a variety of forums since 1999, we have seen across different countries of Europe how teachers, students, administrators, and even some testers, have a dangerous tendency to be satisfied with very little feedback: 'Let's have a batch of good items, delivered quickly and nicely on the Internet, and a result related to CEF levels, that's what we need'.

DIALANG does this, of course, but this is not its main purpose. If it only did this we would be feeding users, but we wouldn't be teaching them how to feed themselves. Going only for the answers to the items and having a look at how many were right or wrong should not be seen as enough any longer. It is to be hoped that systems like DIALANG will become more commonplace in diagnostic testing and will contribute—with the dissemination of, for example, the European Language Portfolio—to learners' gradually developing the capacity for reflection and self-assessment so that they can assume more and more responsibility for their own learning—a necessary tool for citizens in multilingual and plurilingual Europe to acquire.

To conclude, two thoughts on the use of the CEF. First of all, DIALANG proves that the CEF is usable and worth using in the field of language assessment. And second, the feedback gathered on DIALANG, whether it comes from students, from teachers, or from professionals in the field, suggests that it has indeed already contributed to the dissemination of the principles and the levels of the CEF.

References

Alderson, C., C. Clapham, and **D. Wall.** 1995. *Language Test Construction and Evaluation.* Cambridge: Cambridge University Press.

Council of Europe. 2001. *Common European Framework of Reference for Languages.* Cambridge: Cambridge University Press.

DIALANG. web site: www.dialang.org.

Ellis, G. and **B. Sinclair.** 1989. *Learning to Learn English.* Cambridge: Cambridge University Press.

Holec, H. 1980. *Autonomy and Foreign Language Learning.* Strasbourg: Council of Europe.

Huhta, A., S. Luoma, M. Oscarson, K. Sajavaara, S. Takala, and **A. Teasdale.** 2002. **DIALANG – A diagnostic language assessment system for learners** in J. C. Alderson (ed.). *Common European Framework of Reference for Languages: Learning, Teaching, Assessment. Case Studies.* Strasbourg: Council of Europe.

Kohonen, V. 1999. 'Authentic assessment in affective foreign language education' in A. Jane (ed.). *Affect in Language Learning.* Cambridge: Cambridge University Press: 279–94.

Naiman, N., M. Frolich, D. Stern, and **A. Todesco.** 1978. *The Good Language Learner.* Ontario: Ontario Institute for Studies in Education.

North, B. 1995. 'The development of a common framework scale of language proficiency. Based on a theory of measurement'. PhD Thesis. Thames Valley University.

O'Malley, J. M. and **A. Chamot.** 1990. *Learning Strategies in Second Language Acquisition.* Cambridge: Cambridge University Press.

Oscarsson, M. 1997. 'Self-assessment of foreign and second language proficiency' in C. Clapham and D. Corson (eds.). *The Encyclopaedia of Language and Education.* Volume 7. (Language

Testing and Assessment). Dordrecth: Kluwer Academic Publishers: 175–87.

Oskarsson, M. 1980. *Approaches to Self-Assessment in Foreign Language Learning*. Oxford: Pergamon.

Oxford, R. 1990. *Language Learning Strategies: What Every Teacher Should Know*. New York: Newbury House.

Rubin, J. 1975. 'What the good language learner can teach us'. *TESOL Quarterly* 9: 41–51.

Spolsky, B. 1992. 'The gentle art of diagnostic testing revisited' in E. Shohamy and A. R. Walton (eds.). *Language Assessment for Feedback: Testing and Other Strategies*. Dubuque: Kendall/Hunt: 29–41.

van Lier, L. 1996. *Interaction in the Language Curriculum: Awareness, Autonomy and Authenticity*. London: Longman.

Wenden, A. 1991. *Learner Strategies for Learner Autonomy*. London: Prentice Hall.

Werlich, E. 1988. *A Student's Guide to Text Production*. Berlin: Cornelsen Verlag.

The authors

Ari Huhta works as a researcher at the Centre for Applied Language Studies at the University of Jyväskylä, Finland. He specializes in foreign and second language assessment, and has participated in a number of national and international research and development projects in the field. He has been an active member in the DIALANG project since its start in 1996/7.

Neus Figueras Casanovas works in the local Ministry of Education in Catalonia (Spain), where she is in charge of planning, developing, and administering foreign language certificate exams to adult learners of seven different languages. She has published widely in the field of EFL methodology, testing, and teacher education in Spain and elsewhere in Europe. She has been involved in a number of European projects (Speakeasy, Dialang, Ceftrain) and is one of the members of the Authoring Group commissioned by the Council of Europe to develop a 'Manual for relating examinations to the CEF'.

Relating assessments, examinations, and courses to the CEF

Brian North

Overview

This chapter seeks to demonstrate that the CEF descriptors offer a practical, accessible tool that can be used:

- to relate course, assessment, and examination content to the CEF categories and levels (Specification)
- in conjunction with the CEF Reference video and calibrated reading tasks and items, to train teachers, assessors, and item writers in a standard interpretation of the CEF levels (Standardization)
- to provide criteria for ratings by trained teachers/assessors that can act as an external criterion in order to empirically validate the link to CEF levels (External validation).

The CEF descriptors

Two components are at the core of the CEF. These are the descriptive scheme, which defines activities and qualities of language, and the common reference levels, which define proficiency in as many of these categories as possible on scales at six levels (A1, A2, B1, B2, C1, C2).[1]

A key idea always present in the development of the CEF was to use the descriptor scales in Chapter 4 ('Language use and the language user') and Chapter 5 ('The user/learner's competences') to profile the content of courses, assessments, and examinations. These can then be related to each other through their CEF profile without making direct comparisons between them, or claiming that one is an exact equivalent of the other. The CEF provides nearly 50 descriptor scales to assist in this profiling: 34 for different communicative language activities, and another 13 for aspects of the learner's proficiency. A list of these is set out in Reference document 5, 'CEF sub-scales', in the Reference documents section of this book.

This aim of using a range of sub-scales to profile the content of assessments and examinations is easier to achieve if the descriptors within these scales are clear, unambiguous, and relatively concrete descriptions that are interpreted in a similar way in different contexts.

The CEF descriptors were developed and validated in some 32 workshops with teachers, and then mathematically scaled on the basis of the way teachers interpreted them when they were using them to assess learners in their classes (North 1995, 2000a, 2002a; North and Schneider 1998; Schneider and North 2000). Independent follow-up studies have confirmed that the descriptors can be used in a relatively consistent way in relation to different languages and educational contexts, and when used for self-assessment (Jones 2002; North 2002b; Kaftandjieva and Takala 2002).

Comparing assessments

The fundamental problem in making links between different assessments is the fact that:

- different assessments generally test different things
- each result is reported in terms of the achievement in that particular assessment.

The way around this problem is through setting assessment standards in what is referred to in the UK as 'standards-oriented assessment' (Gipps 1994) and in the USA as 'standards-based assessment' (Messick 1995). The standards are based on a student model—'a simplified description of selected aspects of the infinite varieties of skills and knowledge that characterise real students' (Mislevy 1995: 343). The set of CEF descriptor scales represents such a student proficiency model. There are two types of standards (Messick 1995: 6):

- Content standards, which specify the kinds of things a learner should know and be able to do. Here the CEF descriptive scheme offers a generic scheme against which one can map the content standards of existing tests and from which one can develop content standards for new tests. This mapping process is called 'specification'.
- Performance standards, which define the level of competence a learner should attain at key stages of developing expertise in the knowledge and skills specified by the content standards. Here the CEF common reference levels offer a generic set of defined key stages for many of the categories of the descriptive scheme, against which one can map the performance standards of existing tests, and from which one can develop performance standards for new tests. Ensuring consistent interpretation of the performance standards is called 'standardization'.

Specification

Specification involves studying relevant CEF scales, stating what is and what is not assessed, and what level of achievement is expected. The result can be mapped in a graphic profile, such as the example in Figure 1.

This is a profile of a continuous assessment task for Dutch as a Foreign Language used in Belgium. It is based on a thematically linked integrated skills module.[2] There is a listening task, a reading task, and two speaking

Brian North

Overall	Listening	Reading	Social conver- sation	Information exchange	Notes, messages, and forms	Sociolinguistic	Pragmatic	Linguistic
C2								
C1								
B2+								
B2								
B1+								
B1								
A2+								
A2								
A1								
Overall	Listening	Reading	Social conver- sation	Information exchange	Notes, messages, and forms	Sociolinguistic	Pragmatic	Linguistic

FIGURE 1 Graphic profile of the relationship of assessment components to the CEF levels.

tasks, one of which is an information exchange, and the other a role-played social situation. The only writing is to note information from the information exchange task. The assessment criteria reflect sociolinguistic competence (appropriateness of language), pragmatic competence (message precision, fluency), and linguistic competence (accuracy).

A study of the CEF descriptors indicates that the assessment is basically at Level A2, though a slightly higher level (A2+) is required in Listening and Reading.

The '+' level is interesting. At levels A2, B1 and B2, the CEF descriptor scales generally define levels of achievement above the criterion level yet below the next criterion level, and the labels A2+, B1+, or B2+ are given to these. There is a qualitative shift in what is described at each of the six criterion levels (A1, A2, B1, B2, C1, C2) whereas the difference between a criterion level (e.g. A2) and its plus level (e.g. A2+) reflects a better performance at what is basically the same thing. (For more information, please see the CEF Section 3.6: 'Content coherence in common reference levels', pp. 33–6 of the English version.) These 'plus levels' can be very useful when profiling the standard demanded by an examination, or the level attained by an individual.

Language examination providers

Such a graphic profile in relation to *relevant* categories of the CEF is the outcome of the recommended set of specification procedures put forward in a preliminary pilot version of a 'Manual for relating language examinations to the CEF' that has recently been produced by a team coordinated by the current author (Council of Europe 2003).[3] Reference document 1a in this book is Form A23 in that publication. Users are encouraged to complete various forms giving information about the examination, to follow a procedure considering the range of communicative language activities and the range of aspects of language competence involved, and to report the result in terms of a profile like Figure 1 on page 2.

The precise specification procedure defined in the Manual asks users to provide:
- a general description of the examination
- a more detailed profile in relation to the CEF.

General description of the examination
Here the examination provider is asked to include information about the objectives, the needs of the learner population, the domains and communicative activities tested, the types of tasks used, plus brief details on aspects such as the test development and analysis processes, marking, grading, etc.

Detailed profile of the content in relation to the CEF
Then the examination provider is asked to consider each major CEF category in turn, firstly the different 'communicative language activities' (CEF Chapter 4) and then 'aspects of communicative language competence' (CEF Chapter 5). The types of form used are illustrated in Figure 2 (for communicative language activities) and Figure 3 (for aspects of communicative language competence).

Spoken Interaction	Short description and/or reference
Which situation, content categories, domains are the test takers expected to show ability in? - Table 5 in CEF 4.1 might be of help as a reference	
Which communication themes are the test takers expected to be able to handle? - The lists in CEF 4.2 might be of help as a reference	
⋯ etc ⋯	
After reading the scale for Overall Spoken Interaction, indicate and justify at which level of the scale you would situate your paper. - The sub-scales for spoken interaction in CEF 4.4.3.1. under the scale might be of help as a reference	**Level** **Justification (incl. reference to documentation)**

FIGURE 2   Extract from Manual Form A11: Spoken Interaction.

Linguistic Competence	Short description and/or reference
What is the range of lexical and grammatical competence that the test takers are expected to be able to handle? ■ The lists in CEF 5.2.1.1 and 5.2.1.2 might be of help as a reference	
What is the range of phonological and orthographic competence that the test takers are expected to be able to handle? ■ The lists in CEF 5.2.1.4 and 5.2.1.5 might be of help as a reference	
After reading the scales for Range and Accuracy, indicate and justify at which level of the scale you would situate your examination. ■ The scales for Phonological Control in CEF 5.2.1.4 and for Orthographic Control in 5.2.1.5 might also be of help as a reference	**Level** **Justification (incl. reference to documentation)**
Sociolinguistic Competence	**Short description and/or reference**
etc. – parallel to questions for linguistic competence	

FIGURE 3 Extract from Manual Form A20: Aspects of Language Competence in Spoken Interaction.

In the left-hand column of Figures 2 and 3 there are questions with references to relevant CEF table(s) or list(s). In the right-hand column users are asked to give a short description and reference. In the document, the relevant CEF scale is reproduced with a list of other relevant subscales. Users are asked to indicate and justify at which CEF level the test tasks concerned should be situated. Only those forms that are relevant to the content assessed should be used.

It would be fair to say that claims made by examination boards of equivalences to the CEF that exist at the time of writing are, with one or two exceptions,[4] produced by processes less systematic than the kind of specification procedures described. As is often the case with the projects of the Language Policy Division of the Council of Europe, the Manual is an awareness-raising tool intended to contribute to the spreading of expertise in the area of linking assessments.

Language course providers

Language schools and publishers may wish to consider how the courses they provide relate to the CEF. Here the process is less formalized, but EAQUALS (European Association for Quality Language Services: www.eaquals.org) require their member schools to demonstrate the relationship of their system of levels, assessment, and certification.

One way to do this is to take the following steps:

Levels
- Consult the CEF descriptor scales, and the summary of the CEF levels given as document 1a in the Reference documents section of this book. This incorporates insights into the difference in the emerging competences of the learner at different stages (CEF: pp. 33–6; North 2000a: 271–309).
- Formalize an impression of the way course levels relate to the CEF.

Objectives
- List the CEF descriptors at each level—or take the self-assessment checklists from an appropriate version of the European Language Portfolio that presents these in lists per level. (See the chapter in this book by Peter Lenz for more information about portfolios.)
- Analyse the language tasks, functions, grammatical structures, and vocabulary areas implied in each descriptor.
- Collate and summarize this cross-referencing into a list of tasks, a list of functions, a list of grammatical structures, and a list of vocabulary areas and items.
- Prioritize the lists and incorporate the content into curriculum documents.

This was the process Eurocentres went through internally for English, and the result is published as a 'Level Summary' in the classroom. The Goethe Institute have commissioned a more systematic version for German on a CD-ROM called 'Profile Deutsch'.

Assessments
- Consult the CEF scales for communicative language activities (CEF Chapter 4) to develop a specification for the kinds of assessment tasks, e.g. a speaking assessment ought to encompass both sustained spoken production and spontaneous spoken interaction.
- Use the list of objectives to develop a specification for tests of linguistic competences.

For tests of speaking and writing, consult the CEF scales for aspects of language proficiency (CEF Chapter 5) to define the performance standard, i.e. assessment criteria, for relevant levels. Here a number of approaches are possible, including the following:

All levels
If all levels from beginners to advanced are involved then existing CEF Reference instruments could be used. CEF Table 3 'Qualitative aspects of spoken language use', given as Reference document 4 in the Reference documents section of this book, could be used for spoken tests. This criteria grid provides descriptors for each level for Range, Accuracy, Fluency, Interaction, and Coherence. There is also a scale for pronunciation ('Phonological Control': CEF p. 117) that could be added.

Alternatively, one could use an adapted version for different types of assessment task.

- A spoken interaction task could be assessed with Range, Accuracy, Fluency, Interaction from CEF Table 3, plus the overall scale for 'Overall Spoken Interaction' (CEF p. 74).
- A spoken production task could be assessed with Range, Accuracy, Fluency, Coherence from CEF Table 3, plus the overall scale for 'Overall Production Interaction' (CEF p. 74).

This is the approach taken in the assessment grid for written tasks included in the Manual for relating examinations to the CEF. This is given as Reference document 6 in the reference documents section of this book. This time there are three qualitative criteria to be applied to all texts: Range, Coherence, Accuracy. Then there is a holistic scale 'Overall' to be applied to all texts. Finally, there are scales for 'Description' and for 'Argument' to be applied in tasks requiring those texts-types.

Restricted range of levels
If only a restricted level range is relevant, e.g. B1 to B2, then one could imagine an assessment grid focusing just on those levels, using descriptors for the 'plus' levels in between, where these are available. One could also create other, non-defined, bands of proficiency if desired, as sketched below:
- Grade 6: Strong B2 or above
- Grade 5: B2 descriptor
- Grade 4: Not defined
- Grade 3: B1+ descriptor
- Grade 2: Not defined
- Grade 1: B1 descriptor
- Grade 0: Below B1

However, even when one has defined content standards and performance standards in relation to CEF descriptors, one has not yet considered how the performances on the assessment tasks will be interpreted by the teachers or examiners in practice. Some people are stricter than others. When standards-oriented assessment is put into practice, standardization of people's interpretations of the standard is necessary (Gipps 1994).

Standardization

Standardization of judgements is the second set of procedures put forward in the Manual. All examination providers have some form of:
- standardization training with performance samples for 'productive skills', used to train examiners in reasonably consistent application of the assessment criteria.
- standard-setting and item-writer training procedures for 'receptive skills', used to ensure a reasonably consistent level of difficulty in the tasks and items set.

The Manual strongly recommends that work be done in a logical order:
- Productive skills are easier to work with than receptive skills because one can see the performances being evaluated, and one can relate those performances directly to relevant CEF descriptors. One cannot see a listening or reading performance. Therefore, speaking or writing should be tackled first to standardize the interpretation of CEF levels.

- Reading is easier to work with than listening because although one cannot see the reading performance (only a trace of it with responses on paper or mouse clicks) one can see what is being read.
- Listening is more difficult because the text must be remembered, and because a transcript doesn't reflect delivery features that are integral in determining the difficulty of the task in relation to the text in question.

The Manual puts forward four standardization stages, which are all forms of assessor training:

Stage 1: Familiarization. Exercises in sorting CEF descriptors in order to become familiar with the style of description, with the categories and above all with the levels.

Stage 2: Training. Using calibrated samples[5] to arrive on an interpretation of the CEF levels in common with the interpretation arrived at in other institutions. Two types of calibrated sample are provided.

a CEF Reference video: training with calibrated video recordings of spoken performance.

b CEF Reference items: training with calibrated reading test tasks and items.

Training starts with 'illustration' with the calibrated samples, in which the trainer helps participants to relate the performances to the criteria given. This is followed by practice in pairs, followed by discussion. Finally, there is a phase of individual assessment, followed by discussion.

Stage 3: Benchmarking. Using the common interpretation of the CEF levels arrived at by using the calibrated performances on video to benchmark local performance samples to CEF levels. This is best done in a second session, in which some of the CEF calibrated samples are replayed, and then the co-ordinator switches to local video recordings. The CEF Reference video acts as a catalyst for 'piggybacking' to a set of local CEF Reference samples. 'Local' here can mean a country, an educational sector, or another language.

Stage 4: Standard-setting. Using the common interpretation of the CEF levels arrived at by training with the calibrated tasks and items to estimate the CEF level of local items. This then provides a provisional conversion table transforming scores on the test in question to CEF levels.

Standard-setting, however, is a notoriously difficult business. Initial estimates of the level of difficulty of a task or item often bear a limited relationship to the actual difficulty in practice. Of course, estimates of difficulty err in both directions, and so things sometimes cancel themselves out. But in any assessment that is providing a national or international qualification, empirical validation of this standard-setting is a requirement.

Calibrated samples for standardization training

Two types of calibrated samples are provided for the standardization training in Stage 2 above: learner performances rated onto CEF levels; and test items of a difficulty calibrated to CEF levels.

Brian North

CEF Reference video:

At the time of writing a documented video of performances confirmed as calibrated to CEF levels exists only for English, showing recordings of Swiss adult learners (North and Hughes 2003). A video showing Finnish students at levels B1–B2 for several languages in a school assessment context, plus a video showing English samples at different levels from the University of Cambridge Local Examinations Syndicate, should be available during 2004.

CEF Reference items:

At the time of writing, a CD of reading items for English is available. The items come from UCLES, DIALANG, and the Finnish national authorities. Only reading items are provided at this stage.

The DIALANG and Finnish items are multiple choice. The DIALANG items are discrete (=one text with one item) because they are delivered on computer. The Finnish items also include testlets (=one text with several items).

The UCLES items are taken from the Cambridge ESOL main suite of examinations. At low levels there are some tasks with a very short text, often with an illustration, and one item. Generally, though, there are a range of item types that correspond more closely to the types of reading tasks found in didactic materials (scanning, matching, ordering, etc.).

Empirical validation

Empirical validation, the third and final set of procedures put forward in the Manual, involves the collection and analysis of data on test scores/grades, marker/rater behaviour and other aspects of the assessment in practice. There are two aspects to empirical validation:

- internal validation: concerned with the quality of the test in its own right
- external validation: corroborating the provisional conversion of test scores or assessment ratings to CEF levels that were arrived at on the basis of the benchmarking and standard-setting described above in Standardization.

Although empirical validation is mainly something examination providers are concerned with, schools can also apply basic principles of empirical validation in a simple way. Data analysis for external validation can be carried out satisfactorily with nothing more elaborate than the simple correlation functions in Microsoft Excel and a couple of Microsoft Word tables. Examination providers will no doubt wish to go into more detail, and the Manual provides a Reference supplement should they need advice on how to do so.

Internal validation

Internal validation can be carried out with both qualitative methods, questionnaires, interviews, discourse analysis of language generated, verbal reports on the processes test-takers followed, etc., and quantitative methods, e.g. facility values, reliability theory, factor analysis, item response theory, etc. An approach balancing both qualitative and quantitative validation can be recommended.

External validation addresses aspects of the question: 'Does a CEF result reported by this assessment relate to the common interpretation of CEF levels with an acceptable degree of consistency?'

- Do the procedures used to set 'cut-off scores' for different CEF levels function properly?
- Is the interpretation of the CEF levels comparable to interpretations elsewhere?
- Is there any independent verification that results reported onto the CEF levels from this assessment relate reasonably to results for the same people reached by another assessment for the same skill(s)?
- If Portuguese learners of French were to take a Swedish test for French, would they get the CEF levels as when they take their Portuguese test of French?
- … and so on.

External validation

The rest of this section will focus on external validation: corroborating the claimed link to the CEF levels. This aspect is of interest to course providers as well as examination providers.

The external criterion could be either a test of the same skill(s) already calibrated to the CEF, or judgements by teachers who know the learners' work well, and who have been systematically trained in a standardized interpretation of the CEF levels. All learners operating as subjects need to take both the assessment under study and the assessment used as an external criterion.

Step 1: Correlation. A correlation coefficient between the two sets of scores should be calculated. This is not difficult. One can put the two sets of scores into two columns in Microsoft Excel, and select the CORR function. A weak correlation coefficient, e.g. 0.40, shows a weak relationship between the two assessments. There is little point in proceeding further. A relatively strong correlation, e.g. 0.80, shows a very promising relationship between the two assessments. The actual significance of the size of the correlation coefficient depends upon the number of subjects.

Step 2: Matching classifications. A correlation shows that there is a relationship. The next question is what precisely that relationship is. A table can be constructed that compares the level classification for each person on the assessment under study and on the assessment taken as a criterion measure.

A very simple example of this technique is given in Figure 4. The figure comes from North (2000b) and shows how teacher judgements were used to confirm provisional cut-off points between levels on the Eurocentres Scale of Language Proficiency for an item bank testing systemic knowledge of German. Both sets of results are presented in terms of levels on the Eurocentres scale, not the CEF. The study is illustrated here only as a published methodological example. The results on the two assessments are simply plotted against each other in a Microsoft Word table. It helps to then shade the diagonal line—which is where all the learners would be if the correlation between the two assessments was absolutely perfect.

Item banke r	1	2	3	4	5	6	7	8	9
9								2	
8								1	
7							8	3	
6					2		8		
5				1	8	2	1		
4			4		4				
3		2	6	5					
2	1	1	5						
1	4								

Teacher Judgement: *Sprachkenntisse*

FIGURE 4 Referencing an item bank to teacher judgements.

In this example, the relationship between the two sets of results appears regular. However, despite the very high correlation of 0.93, only 28 of the 68 subjects (41%) were actually placed at the same level out of the nine Eurocentres levels by both the item bank and the teachers. There are eight learners placed at Level 7 by the teacher(s) and Level 6 by the programme. This was caused by a generous teacher. However, even if these 8 test takers were in 'the right place' on the chart still only about 50% of the students would have received exactly the same rating from the teacher and the test.

Part of the reason why so few learners have received the same classification concerns the number of levels on the scale. The Eurocentres scale splits each CEF level other than A1 and C2 into two (see North 2000a: 337 for an explanation) to give 9 levels overall. Thus Eurocentres Levels 2 and 3 make A2; Levels 4 and 5 make B1; Levels 6 and 7 make B2, and Levels 8 and 9 make C1. There were no learners in this sample at C2.

For this reason, the Manual recommends that, whatever set of finer level classifications may be used locally, only the official six CEF levels A1–C2 should be used when comparing assessments. The Manual suggests making what it describes as a 'Decision table'. Such a 'Decision table' using only CEF levels for exactly the same set of data as used for Figure 4 is shown in Figure 5. Again, this is simply a Microsoft Word table. Using only the CEF levels, as in Figure 5, the proportion of common classifications increases to 50 out of 68.

Following the 'Decision Table' format, the assessment under study (the test bank) is put across the top, and the assessment used as an external criterion (the teacher judgements) is put down on the left-hand side. Thus the four learners at Eurocentres Level 1, CEF Level A1, are now in the top right-hand corner rather than in the bottom left corner, as on Figure 4. With the exception of Level 1, the numbered Eurocentres levels are now also paired into the CEF levels. Thus 14 learners have now been placed at Level A2 (Eurocentres 2 and 3) by both test bank and teachers, 13 are now placed by both at Level B1 (Eurocentres 4 and 5) etc.

The margins on the right and at the bottom, outside the box, just give totals. The total number of subjects, 68, can thus be seen in the bottom right-hand corner.

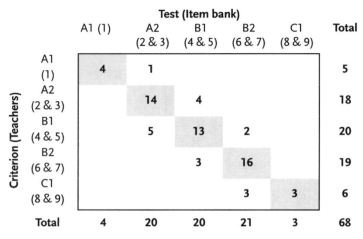

		Test (Item bank)					
		A1 (1)	A2 (2 & 3)	B1 (4 & 5)	B2 (6 & 7)	C1 (8 & 9)	Total
Criterion (Teachers)	A1 (1)	4	1				5
	A2 (2 & 3)		14	4			18
	B1 (4 & 5)		5	13	2		20
	B2 (6 & 7)			3	16		19
	C1 (8 & 9)				3	3	6
	Total	4	20	20	21	3	68

FIGURE 5 Figure 4 as a CEF Manual 'Decision table'.

Step 3: Calculating the proportion of common classifications. The proportion of common classifications is expressed as a simple percentage. In the case being discussed, the teachers and the provisional cut-offs in the item bank produced common classifications onto the CEF levels in 50 out of 68=73.5% of the cases.

A common classification of 73.5% between two independent assessments is a very good result indeed. In this particular case, these teachers knew the Eurocentres scale very well as they had been working with it for several years. They taught their small classes for at least 15 hours a week, and so also knew the students very well. The items in the item bank had been written to a tight specification for each level, and less reliable or badly targeted items had already been removed during development.

By contrast, Schneider and North (2000) report severe problems using teacher ratings in relation to less familiar descriptors by Swiss teachers seeing classes only a couple of hours a week. The same problem occurred in a large-scale placement testing procedure Eurocentres tried in Brazil in 1997 and 1998. In these cases, it became clear that some teachers really could not distinguish between the proficiency of individual learners in large classes that they only saw twice a week.

For the approach to work, it is important that teachers are fully trained in the levels with the reference video, really know the students well, and are trained in standards-based assessment. It doesn't hurt to try, though. The worst that can happen is a low correlation. In such a case one doesn't know who is right and who is wrong—or whether both are wrong. But with a reasonable correlation, one has a relationship between the two assessments. Then one can plot the 'Decision Table' to find out precisely what it is.

One can draw three conclusions from the above example:

- Firstly, the study discussed here was a very simple study, involving little logistical organization and virtually no expense. Yet the 'pay-off' in terms of confirmation of the standard-setting adopted in the item bank was considerable.
- Secondly, as mentioned above, the calculation of a correlation coefficient can be done in Microsoft Excel, which offers two formulae, CORREL and PEARSON, for this purpose. The graphic plotting techniques employed in both figures used to display the results can be done, as above, with a Microsoft Word table. Thus, since nothing more sophisticated than Microsoft Office is required, this sort of external validation ought to be well within the reach of even those language professionals who do not think of themselves as particularly numerate.
- Thirdly, when plotting decision agreement to the criterion for the purposes of external validation to the CEF, only full CEF levels should be used. Using finer levels (as Eurocentres do) may be pedagogically meaningful, but in a testing context it requires a higher degree of decision power. This is why 'high stakes' assessment (examinations) tend to use broad levels in order to reduce the number of misclassifications. This is also why the CEF and the European Language Portfolio—a formal reporting instrument—have only six levels.

Conclusion

The CEF has an ambitious aim. It tries to provide a transparent and coherent framework that can be shared by language professionals (schools, examination providers, publishers) learners (especially through the Portfolio) and wider stake holders (parents, employers, ministries, international bodies). The self-assessment descriptor grid from the Portfolio (CEF Table 2 given as Document 2 in the Reference documents section of this book) is incorporated in the language section of the European Union's EUROPASS, that is intended to be a simple instrument reporting achievement in professional training.

The approach taken in the Manual for relating language examinations to the CEF is presented in such a way as to encourage examination providers, schools and networks of teachers using the Portfolio to all use the same principles to relate their assessments to the CEF. Many institutions are taking part in 2004–5 in case studies piloting the new Manual in order to validate the linking of their assessments to the CEF. The CEF and the Manual associated with it are open-ended instruments. The current edition of the CEF, the current set of descriptors, the current Manual, the current reference video will all be supplemented and revised. Any feedback and offers of piloting is very welcome, and can be addressed to Johanna.Panthier@coe.int.

Notes

1 The CEF was developed by an authoring group consisting of John Trim, Daniel Coste, Brian North, and Joe Sheils under the supervision of an international working party between 1993 and 1996. The revision for the 2000 published version was undertaken by John Trim and Brian North.

2 Further information about the assessment can be obtained from Piet van Avermaet of the University of Leuven on piet.vanavermaet@arts.kuleuven.ac.be.

3 The Manual was developed by an authoring group consisting of Brian North, Neus Figueras, Piet Van Avermaet, Norman Verhelst, and Sauli Takala with assistance from a sounding board of consultants.

4 At the time of writing, the University of Cambridge Local Examinations Syndicate, the DIALANG project for web-based tests, and the Finnish national examination authority have followed a principled procedure to link their assessments to the CEF. TOEIC, TOEFL, and City and Guilds/Pitmans ESOL, are known to be planning such a process.

5 For information about the latest calibrated samples and how to order them, please refer to the website of the Language Policy Division at http://culture.coe.int/lang.

References

Alderson, J. C. A. (ed.). 2002. *Case Studies in applying the Common European Framework* Strasbourg: Council of Europe.

Council of Europe. 2001. *Common European Framework of Reference for Languages: Learning, Teaching, Assessment.* Cambridge: Cambridge University Press.
Also available for download from http://www.coe.int/T/E/Cultural_Co-operation/education/Languages/Language_Policy/Common_Framework_of_Reference/1cadre.asp#TopOfPage

Council of Europe. 2003. *Relating Language Examinations to the Common European Framework of Reference for Languages: Learning, Teaching, Assessment (CEF). Preliminary Pilot Version of a Proposed Manual.* DGIV/EDU/LANG (2003) 5, Strasbourg. September 2003.

Gipps, C. 1994. *Beyond Testing.* London: The Falmer Press.

Jones, N. 2002. 'Relating the ALTE framework to the Common European Framework of Reference' in J. C. A. Alderson (ed.): 167–83.

Kaftandjieva, F. and **S. Takala.** 2002. 'Council of Europe scales of language proficiency, a validation study' in J. C. A. Alderson (ed.): 106–29.

Messick, S. M. 1995. 'Standards of validity and the validity of standards in performance assessment' *Educational Measurement: Issues and Practice*, 14/4: *Special Issue: Values and Standards in Performance Assessment: Issues, Findings and Viewpoints* 5–8.

Mislevy, R. J. 1995. 'Test theory and language learning assessment'. *Language Testing* 12/3: 341–69.

North, B. 1995. 'The development of a common framework scale of descriptors of language proficiency based on a theory of measurement'. *System* 23/4: 445–65.

North, B. 2000a. *The Development of a Common Framework Scale of Language Proficiency.* New York: Peter Lang.

North, B. 2000b. 'Linking language assessments: an example in a low-stakes context'. *System* 28/4: 555–77.

North, B. 2002a. 'Developing descriptor scales of language proficiency for the CEF common reference levels' in J. C. A. Alderson (ed.): 87–105.

North, B. 2002b. 'A CEF-based self-assessment tool for university entrance' in J. C. A. Alderson (ed.): 87–105.

North, B. and **G. Hughes.** 2003. *CEF Performance Samples: for Relating Language Examinations to the Common European Framework of Reference for Languages: Learning, Teaching, Assessment. English. Swiss Adult Learners.* Council of Europe, Eurocentres, Migros Club Schools. Video cassette.

North, B. and **G. Schneider.** 1998. 'Scaling descriptors for language proficiency scales'. *Language Testing* 15/2: 217–62.

Schneider, G. and **North, B.** 2000. *Fremdsprachen können—was heisst das? Skalen zur Beschreibung, Beurteilung und Selbsteinschätzung der fremdsprachlichen Kommunikationsfähigkeit.* Chur/Zürich: Verlag Rüeger.

The author

Brian North is Head of Academic Development at Eurocentres, where he developed the Eurocentres scale of language proficiency and assessment approach. He is one of the authors of the CEF and of the prototype European Language Portfolio. He developed the CEF levels and descriptor scales in his PhD as part of a national research project in Switzerland. He is currently coordinating the work of the Council of Europe in connection with relating language examinations to the CEF.

Using the CEF to develop an ESL curriculum for newcomer pupils in Irish primary schools

David Little and Barbara Lazenby Simpson

Overview

This chapter reports on the use of the Common European Framework in a project to develop an ESL curriculum for newcomer pupils in Irish primary schools. It begins by summarizing the background to the project, then deals in turn with the three phases of the project to date:

1 the initial development of English language proficiency benchmarks and a version of the European Language Portfolio based closely on them (2000)

2 the development and introduction of a wide range of related supports for ESL teachers and their pupils (2000–3)

3 the revision of the English language proficiency benchmarks in the light of three years' experience and with an eye to future developments (2003).

Background

Since the early 1990s, increasing numbers of migrants have come to Ireland. Although the rights and entitlements of adults vary according to their legal status, their children are expected to attend school, which means that they must be taught English. In 2000 the Department of Education and Science (DES) commissioned Integrate Ireland Language and Training (IILT), a not-for-profit campus company of Trinity College Dublin, to develop a project to support ESL teachers in primary and post-primary (i.e. second level) schools. Although both sectors have been served by the same project, this chapter concentrates on primary level, partly for clarity's sake and partly because that is where we have done most work. The challenge to which our project is a response may be summarized as follows:

■ Newcomer pupils may arrive at any time in the school year.

■ At primary level they may be any age between 4½ and 12.

■ They may have some English, very little English, or no English at all.

■ They may have no previous educational experience, either because of their age (in many countries of origin schooling begins only at the age of 6 or 7) or as a result of previous circumstances (they may have come, for example, from a war zone or have spent extended periods of time in transit camps). If they have already attended school, they will

have at least some familiarity with the concept of literacy; but their previous experience of reading and writing may have involved a writing system other than the Roman alphabet.
- Those who have come to Ireland as refugees may be suffering from some kind of trauma.

The domestic circumstances of newcomer pupils are almost infinitely variable. At one extreme they may be the children of professional parents who place a high value on educational success; at the other they may be the children of asylum seekers living in communal accommodation where it is practically impossible to find a quiet space in which to do homework. Children in the former category usually have no difficulty in establishing social contact with their peers outside school; those in the latter category sometimes have no contact with native-English speakers except at school.

The number of newcomer pupils in a school may be very low, as few as four or five; or it may be as many as a 100, so that newcomer pupils comprise a significant proportion of the school's population. Even when a school has only a handful of newcomer pupils, they may be drawn from two or more contrasting ethnic backgrounds—for example, children of migrant workers from the Middle East or the Indian sub-continent and children of African refugees. The mother tongues of newcomer pupils may also have little in common—it is not unusual for one school to have native speakers of Arabic, several African languages, and one or more eastern European languages. Precisely how many mother tongues are now represented in Irish primary schools is unknown as there are no official figures. But estimates in the region of 120 are probably not seriously wide of the mark.

When newcomer pupils first arrive at school, they are assigned to a mainstream class, usually on the basis of their age. This is where they spend most of their time. Each pupil is entitled to two years of ESL support, which is provided on a withdrawal basis—pupils being taken out of their mainstream class for usually one or two hours each day. A major function of ESL classes is to find ways of ensuring that pupils continue to learn English when they return from their ESL class to the mainstream. The DES funds ESL support according to the number of newcomer pupils in the school. If there are fewer than 14 newcomers, it makes an allocation per pupil to fund hourly-paid teaching; if there are 14 or more, it funds a full-time teaching post; and if there are 28 or more, it funds two full-time teaching posts. This arrangement means that the more newcomer pupils a school has, the easier it is to develop a flexible system of language support; though some very large primary schools have many more than 28 newcomer pupils but still only two full-time ESL teachers.

Where we started
English language proficiency benchmarks and the European Language Portfolio

Although the DES had been funding ESL support for several years, nothing had been done to define the ESL teacher's task, develop support materials, or provide in-service seminars. Clearly, the first thing we needed was a map of the ground to be covered. As it happened this was already partly drawn. In a report submitted to the DES in 1996 we had recommended that research should be undertaken to 'define proficiency

David Little and Barbara Lazenby Simpson

benchmarks corresponding to the language needs of children and adults in education, vocational training, and everyday life' (Little and Lazenby Simpson 1996: 87); and the terms of reference that the DES laid down for IILT's two-year pilot phase included the elaboration of these benchmarks. They were already beginning to take shape when the DES asked IILT to develop a project for ESL teachers.

Why we used the CEF

Our starting point in elaborating the benchmarks was the second draft of the Common European Framework (Council of Europe 1996). This has substantially the same content as the published version (Council of Europe 2001), but the order of presentation is somewhat different. We decided to use the CEF for two reasons.

First, we badly needed to define stages in ESL development, and the CEF's six common reference levels (A1–C2) offer a detailed and empirically grounded description of progression in second/foreign language learning. As even cursory study of the self-assessment grid reveals, however (See the document 2 in the Reference documents section of this book; also Council of Europe 2001: 26ff.), the common reference levels define a trajectory of adolescent and adult language learning that runs from minimal survival skills to advanced proficiency underpinned by high levels of educational and/or professional attainment. This was more than we needed. The aim of ESL support, limited as it is to two years per pupil, is to bring newcomers to the level of proficiency they require for full participation in mainstream education. For that purpose the first three common reference levels were enough: A1, A2, and B1.

Our second reason for using the CEF had to do with what we take to be its most innovative feature: its use of 'can do' statements to define communicative proficiency. For the same 'can do' statements serve as a basis not only for specifying learning goals, but for selecting and grading learning activities and evaluating learning outcomes. By adopting this approach we hoped to ensure that the benchmarks could be used not only as a map of the ground to be covered but as an outline teaching manual and a set of assessment criteria.

Adapting CEF descriptors

Of course, we could not use the descriptors of the CEF as such; they were inappropriate to the age range of our newcomer pupils, and they lacked a specific educational focus. They had to be reformulated taking account of the varieties of discourse regularly encountered in Irish primary schools and the themes and topics of the Irish primary curriculum. This required us to do two things: to bring the descriptors that define levels A1, A2, and B1 in the CEF into interaction with the primary curriculum; and to draw on the experience of teachers who were already providing ESL support. We did this by establishing two focus groups.

The key elements in the 2000 benchmarks (developed by Fiona O'Connor in consultation with David Little, Barbara Lazenby Simpson, and Eilish Hurley) are:

1 global descriptors of language proficiency at three levels (A1–B1) and in five skills (listening, reading, spoken interaction, spoken production, and writing);

2 fourteen units of work related to the benchmarks: 'Myself'; 'Our school'; 'Food and clothes'; 'Colours, shapes and opposites'; 'People who help us'; 'People and places in other areas'; 'Local and wider community'; 'Caring for my locality'; 'Time'; 'Weather'; 'Transport'; 'Seasons, holidays and festivals'; 'Animals and plants'; 'Water'. See the Appendices to this chapter: Appendix 1—the global descriptors; Appendix 2— the units of work for 'Food and clothes and Weather'.

3 a version of the European Language Portfolio (ELP) developed in parallel with the benchmarks to help teachers and learners to organize their work in a way that explicitly takes account of the progression defined in the benchmarks and the themes and topics elaborated in the units of work. In the language passport section of this ELP newcomer pupils records their linguistic and cultural identity and (usually with the teacher's help) regularly assess their developing proficiency in English against the global descriptors. The language biography contains four pages designed to raise pupils' awareness of language learning and language use, and then a series of self-assessment checklists that correspond to the units of work. The descriptors in the checklist headed 'Myself', for example, are:

> I can talk about myself, my name and my age
> I can talk about the things I like and the things I am good at
> I can talk about my hobbies
> I can talk about my family and what they are doing
> I can explain to my parents what I am doing at school
> I can talk about what I did last year compared to this year

Finally, the dossier section comprises a contents page and a number of worksheets related to the units of work.

Uses of the ELP

The ELP has a reporting and a pedagogical function. It serves as a cumulative record of language learning process and achievement, while its emphasis on goal-setting and self-assessment is designed to encourage reflective learning and support the development of learner autonomy (see the chapter by Peter Lenz in this book; Little and Perclová 2001; Little 2002). Our decision to develop a version of the ELP to use with the benchmarks took account of both functions. Each pupil's ELP would provide the ESL teacher, the mainstream class teacher, the school principal, school inspectors, and parents with a comprehensive overview of progress and achievement in English. At the same time the ELP gave us a practical way of communicating to ESL teachers our own commitment to the pursuit of learner autonomy (Little 1991; Lazenby Simpson 2002, 2003).

Implementation: 2000–3

Having developed the benchmarks and ELP, we began to introduce them in the autumn term of 2000. In each of the past three school years we have offered two in-service seminars for primary ESL teachers. Each seminar has been given five times, in different parts of the country. The

David Little and Barbara Lazenby Simpson

total number of teachers attending each round of seminars has risen steadily and now stands at about 250. At each seminar as many as half the participants are new to ESL teacher support. This is due to two factors: a tendency on the part of many schools to second mainstream class teachers to language support for a limited period only; and the mobility of the newcomer population, which causes some schools to lose their ESL support funding and brings newcomer pupils to other schools for the first time.

Implementation strategy

Our basic strategy for the implementation phase of our project was to use the benchmarks and the ELP as a constant point of reference for describing ESL support, identifying problems, and exploring possible solutions. We already knew from our focus groups that the three-stage approach to the provision of ESL support: Breakthrough (A1), Waystage (A2), and threshold (B1), corresponded to teachers' intuitions; and those intuitions were reinforced by the ELP. The benchmarks and the ELP served as the foundation on which we gradually built an elaborate structure of information, guidelines, reporting and assessment tools, and teaching materials.

Parts of the structure were determined by the nature of the benchmarks and the general pedagogical orientation implied by the ELP. These include:
- a handbook that explains page by page how to use the ELP
- detailed guidelines on the design and implementation of ESL support programmes at the levels of school, class, and individual pupil
- equally detailed guidelines on assessing communicative proficiency as an integral part of the teaching–learning process
- assessment checklists for the units of work, to be used as part of the teacher's record of individual pupil progress.

Other parts of the structure were developed in response to requests from the teachers:
- information sheets on second language acquisition and the 'silent period'
- summaries of the religious beliefs and practices of some migrant groups
- a questionnaire for making an initial assessment of newly arrived ESL pupils
- 80-page guides to the use of mainstream textbooks in ESL classes and the development of literacy in newcomer pupils admitted to senior primary classes.

Other parts of the structure were developed in interaction with the teachers, notably a form that uses icons to communicate with non-English-speaking parents at parent-teacher meetings, a guide to the Irish school system for newcomer parents (to date this has been translated into the ten numerically strongest newcomer languages), and a guide to ESL support for mainstream teachers, school principals, and inspectors.

Lessons from this phase	The benchmarks were deliberately kept simple and rather general in their phrasing in order to make them easily accessible to teachers who were not used to thinking of communicative proficiency and language learning objectives in behavioural terms. There is no doubt that this characteristic helps to explain the remarkable speed and ease with which teachers accepted the benchmarks and began to think about their teaching and their pupils' learning in terms of three stages and five communicative skills. But in time the same characteristic turned out to be a serious limitation, especially when we turned our attention to the problem of developing the literacy skills of older ESL pupils with very little English. Although the global descriptors (Appendix 1) distinguish the five communicative skills of the Common European Framework, the units of work do not (Appendix 2). This means that the benchmarks had too little to contribute to the detailed development of teaching materials and approaches. For the same reason, and self-assessment checklists notwithstanding, the benchmarks could not contribute in a sufficiently precise way to the development of detailed assessment procedures.

Accordingly, in the summer of 2003 we decided to revise the benchmarks. By this time, of course, we could draw on a wealth of experience and information that had not been available to us in 2000.

A new version of the English language proficiency benchmarks: 2003	In revising the benchmarks we had three specific aims in mind:

1 We wanted to define our global scales of communicative proficiency in greater detail than previously, in order to make the progression across the three levels plainer.

2 Our three years of regular contact with teachers had made us aware that in some respects the progression captured by the global scales was not very different from the developmental path followed by native speaker pupils, especially in the first year or two of primary schooling. Accordingly, we wanted to provide a second set of scales that would refer to key features of the linguistic competence that underpins communicative proficiency.

3 We wanted to rewrite the units of work to take account of the five communicative skills, so that they would provide more precise guidance in selecting learning materials and activities and developing assessment procedures.

Stages of the revision,	We put aside the original benchmarks, returned to the CEF, and re-wrote levels A1, A2, and B1 of the self-assessment grid to make them correspond as precisely as possible to the age of our learners and the context of their learning (see Appendix 3).

Next we drew on the scales that deal with various features of linguistic competence to create a scale with four dimensions: vocabulary control, grammatical accuracy, phonological control, and orthographic control (Appendix 4).

Then we worked through all the illustrative scales by means of which the CEF expands on the summary descriptors of the self-assessment grid.

David Little and Barbara Lazenby Simpson

See Document 5 in the Reference documents section of this book for a list of these. We deleted those scales and descriptors that were not relevant to our domain and used those that were left to guide us in rewriting the units of work. We include here the revised versions of 'Food and clothes' and 'Weather' (Appendix 5) for comparison with the earlier versions (Appendix 2).

Conclusion

As should be clear from the account we have given of our project, the CEF and the ELP have proved highly effective support in developing and introducing an ESL curriculum for newcomer pupils in Irish primary schools.

The CEF enabled us to launch our project on the basis of a three-stage development that was grounded in the first three common reference levels but also corresponded to teachers' intuitions; and the ELP quickly established itself as an indispensable tool for teachers and learners (by the summer of 2003 more than 5,000 copies were in circulation). We shall now bring our version of the ELP into line with the revised benchmarks and use the benchmarks to develop more elaborate and precise assessment procedures. By the summer of 2005 we aim to have a fully developed ESL curriculum for newcomer pupils at primary level—benchmarks, ELP, ELP-related teaching materials, assessment procedures, and a handbook for teachers. Every part of the curriculum will be informed by our regular contact with teachers and every part will be fully integrated with the mainstream primary curriculum.

No doubt our project could have followed many different paths from the one we have taken. But after three years we find it difficult to imagine working without the twin supports of the CEF and the ELP.

Note

The 2003 English language proficiency benchmarks and the version of the ELP for newcomer pupils at primary level can be downloaded from the IILT website: www.iilt.ie.

References

Council of Europe. 1996. *Modern Languages: Learning, Teaching, Assessment. A Common European Framework of Reference.* Draft 2 of a Framework proposal. Strasbourg: Council of Europe.
Council of Europe. 2001. *Common European Framework of Reference for Languages: Learning, Teaching, Assessment.* Cambridge: Cambridge University Press. Also available for download from: http://www.coe.int/T/E/Cultural_Cooperation/education/Languages/Language_Policy/Common_Framework_of_Reference/1cadre.asp#TopOfPage.
Lazenby Simpson, B. 2002. 'Meeting the needs of second language children: language and literacy in primary education'. Plenary paper given at the conference of the Reading Association of Ireland, 3–5 October.
Lazenby Simpson, B. 2003. 'Second language learning: providing for immigrant learners'. In D. Little, J. Ridley and E. Ushioda (eds.), *Learner Autonomy in the Foreign Language Classroom: Learner, Teacher, Curriculum and Assessment,* Dublin: Authentik: 198–210.
Little, D. 1991. *Learner Autonomy 1: Definitions, Issues and Problems.* Dublin: Authentik.
Little, D. 2002. 'The European Language Portfolio: structure, origins, implementation and challenges'. *Language Teaching* 35/3: 182–9.
Little, D. and **B. Lazenby Simpson.** 1996. Meeting the language needs of refugees. Unpublished report. Dublin: Trinity College, Centre for Language and Communication Studies.
Little, D. and **R. Perclová.** 2001. *European Language Portfolio: Guide for Teachers and Teacher Trainers.* Strasbourg: Council of Europe. Available online at <culturecoe.int/portfolio>.

The authors

David Little is founding director (1978) of the Centre for Language and Communication Studies and Associate Professor of Applied Linguistics at Trinity College Dublin. He is the author and co-author of several books and numerous articles on the theory and practice of learner autonomy and the use of new technologies in second language learning. He is currently a consultant to the Council of Europe's European Language Portfolio project and director of Integrate Ireland Language and Training, a government-funded unit that provides English language support for newcomers to Ireland.

Barbara Lazenby Simpson has been involved in English language teaching since the early 1970s. She is currently a research fellow at the Centre for Language and Communication Studies, Trinity College Dublin, and deputy director of Integrate Ireland Language and Training. Her work focuses on migrant second language learning from primary school pupils to older adult learners and involves course design, materials development, teacher education and in-career development, and research across the domain. She has been designing and implementing European Language Portfolios since 1998.

Appendix 1 Global descriptors of language proficiency from this project (2000)

		A1 Breakthrough	A2 Waystage	B1 Threshold
Understanding	**Listening** *The pupil can …*	… understand common greetings and everyday expressions of social interaction.	…follow a short familiar concrete story. …follow the main points of a general conversation.	… understand a range of stories and follow other's conversation. … listen carefully, in order to remember and respond.
	Reading *The pupil can …*	… recognize own name. … match words with pictures of common everyday objects. … read short sentences about family and immediate physical surroundings.	… read and use classroom notices, labels, captions, etc. … predict events in stories and read short sentences on familiar topics using semantic or picture cues. … read patterned and predictable text.	… use different strategies for word recognition and identification. … read short texts for pleasure and information gathering.
Speaking	**Spoken interaction** *The pupil can …*	… answer greeting and questions about self, family and immediate physical needs (repetition and assistance from the interlocutor may be required).	… ask and answer questions relating to immediate needs. … talk spontaneously with peers; may not respond to conversational cues.	… explain choices clearly and simply and give reasons for opinions and actions. … explore, develop and clarify ideas.
	Spoken production *The pupil can …*	… repeat phrases and ask one or two word questions. … give an account of everyday activities.	… tell a story from pictures in simple sequence. … play in a role for a period of time.	… talk to different audiences for a variety of purposes, including telling stories, predicting, reporting, describing and explaining.
Writing	**Writing** *The pupil can …*	… copy letters, words, and short sentences from board. … form most letters correctly and attempt to spell words using phonic spelling. … write own name and some personal and family information.	… spell key words accurately. … write in sentences and experiment with recently learned words.	… write short texts for different purposes (e.g. posters, stories, descriptions).

Case study 1

Appendix 2: Sample units of work from this project (2000)

Unit 3 – Food and clothes

	A1 Breakthrough	A2 Waystage	B1 Threshold
Food *The pupil can ...*	... identify and name pictures of familiar foods. ... describe foods using adjectives of taste. ... ask for a meal /item in canteen or sweet-shop. ... categorize, in different ways, foods eaten every day.	... describe favourite dishes using comparatives and adjectives. ... explain food preferences in terms of likes and dislikes. ... read short stories on eating habits, etc.	... discuss and justify food choices. ... explain different stages of food preparation. ... read information on healthy eating and incorporate it into project work.
Clothes *The pupil can ...*	... read names of everyday items of clothing. ... group clothing according to different criteria. ... talk about clothes in relation to self, e.g. past and present, favourite colours, etc.	... describe items of everyday clothing. ... identify and talk about different clothing materials. ... talk about shapes and sizes.	... relate clothing choices to weather. ... compare different clothing materials.

Unit 10 – Weather

	A1 Breakthrough		A2 Waystage		B1 Threshold	
	Lower Primary	Upper Primary	Lower Primary	Upper Primary	Lower Primary	Upper Primary
The weather around us *The pupil can ...*	... listen to and repeat weather chants and rhymes. ... describe the daily weather in basic terms. ... assist in charting weather observations.	... report the day's weather using appropriate vocabulary. ... say what kind of weather s/he prefers for different activities.	... listen to stories about stormy/winter weather, etc. ... recognize and describe some of the effects of weather on people, animals and plants.	... research and write a few lines about the effects of particular types of weather. ... describe an ideal day.	... discuss weather elements of the local natural environment. ... explain how climate affects housing, clothing, and food choices.	... read, and tell others, about how climate affects clothing, housing or living conditions. ...learn weather sayings and relate them to own experience.

David Little and Barbara Lazenby Simpson

Appendix 3 Global benchmarks of communicative proficiency (2003)

Receptive skills

	A1 Breakthrough	A2 Waystage	B1 Threshold
Listening	Can recognize and understand basic words and phrases concerning him/herself, family and school.	Can recognize and understand frequently used words relating to him/herself and family, classroom activities and routines, school instructions and procedures, friends and play.	Can understand the main points of topics that are presented clearly in the mainstream classroom.
	Can understand simple questions and instructions when teachers and other pupils speak very slowly and clearly.	Can understand a routine instruction given outside school (e.g. by a traffic warden).	Can understand the main points of stories that are read aloud in the mainstream classroom.
		Can understand what is said in a familiar context such as buying something in a shop (e.g. price).	Can understand a large part of a short film on a familiar topic provided that it is age-appropriate.
		Can follow at a general level topics covered in the mainstream class provided key concepts and vocabulary have been studied in advance and there is appropriate visual support.	Can understand detailed instructions given in all school contexts (classroom, gym, playground, etc.).
		Can follow and understand a story if it is read slowly and clearly with visual support such as facial expression, gesture and pictures.	Can follow classroom talk between two or more native speakers, only occasionally needing to request clarification.
Reading (if appropriate to the age of the pupil)	Can recognize the letters of the alphabet.	Can read and understand very short and simple texts that contain a high proportion of previously learnt vocabulary on familiar subjects (e.g. class texts, familiar stories).	Can read and understand the main points in texts encountered in the mainstream class, provided the thematic area and key vocabulary are already familiar.
	Can recognize and understand basic signs and simple notices in the school and on the way to school.	Can use the alphabet to find particular items in lists (e.g. a name in a telephone book).	Can read and understand descriptions of events, feelings and wishes.
	Can recognize and understand basic words on labels or posters in the classroom.		Can use comprehension questions to find specific answers in a piece of text.
	Can identify basic words and phrases in a new piece of text.		Can use key words, diagrams and illustrations to support reading comprehension.
			Can follow clearly written instructions (for carrying out a classroom task, assembling or using an object, following directions, etc.).

Understanding

	A1 Breakthrough	A2 Waystage	B1 Threshold
Spoken Interaction	Can greet, say *please* and *thank you*, and ask for directions to another place in the school. Can respond non-verbally to basic directions to a place in the school when the other person supplements speech with signs or gestures. Can give simple answers to basic questions when given time to reply and the other person is prepared to help. Can make basic requests in the classroom or playground (e.g., for the loan of a pencil) and respond appropriately to the basic requests of others.	Can ask for attention in class. Can greet, take leave, request and thank appropriately. Can respond with confidence to familiar questions clearly expressed about family, friends, school work, hobbies, holidays, etc., but is not always able to keep the conversation going. Can generally sustain a conversational exchange with a peer in the classroom when carrying out a collaborative learning activity (making or drawing something, preparing a role-play, presenting a puppet show, etc.). Can express personal feelings in a simple way.	Can speak with fluency about familiar topics such as school, family, daily routine, likes and dislikes. Can engage with other pupils in discussing a topic of common interest (songs, football, pop stars, etc.) or in preparing a collaborative classroom activity. Can keep a conversation going, though he/she may have some difficulty making him/herself understood from time to time. Can repeat what has been said and convey the information to another person.
Spoken Production	Can use simple phrases and sentences to describe where he/she lives and people he/she knows, especially family members.	Can use a series of phrases and sentences to describe in simple terms his/her family, daily routines and activities, and plans for the immediate or more distant future (e.g. out-of-school activities, holiday plans).	Can retell a story that has been read in class. Can retell the plot of a film he/she has seen a book he/she has read and describe his/her reactions. Can describe a special event/celebration in the family (religious festival, birthday, new baby, etc.). Can give an account of an experience or event (travel, an accident, an incident that occurred, etc.). Can briefly give explanations and reasons for opinions and plans.

Speaking

David Little and Barbara Lazenby Simpson

Productive skills — continued

	A1 Breakthrough	A2 Waystage	B1 Threshold
Writing (if appropriate to the age of the pupil)	Can copy or write his/her name.	Can enter newly-learnt terms in a personal or topic-based dictionary, possibly including sample sentences.	Can write a diary or news account with accuracy and coherence.
	Can copy or write words and short phrases that are being learnt in class.	Can write short texts on specific or familiar topics (e.g. what I like to do when I'm at home).	Can write a short letter describing an event or a situation.
	Can copy or write labels on a picture.	Can write a short message (e.g. a postcard) to a friend.	Can write a brief summary of a book or film.
	Can copy short sentences from the board.		Can write an account of his/her feelings or reactions to an event or situation.
	Can spell his/her name and address, and the name of the school.		Can write a short dialogue to be performed by puppets.

Writing

Case study 1

Appendix 4 Global scales of underlying linguistic competence (2003)

	A1 Breakthrough	A2 Waystage	B1 Threshold
Vocabulary control	Can recognize, understand and use a limited range of basic vocabulary which has been used repeatedly in class or has been specifically taught.	Can recognize, understand and use a range of vocabulary associated with concrete everyday needs or learning experiences (e.g. topics or routines that have been introduced and practised in class).	Can recognize, understand and use a range of vocabulary related to familiar classroom themes, school routines and activities. Errors still occur when the pupil attempts to express more complex ideas or handle unfamiliar topics.
Grammatical accuracy	Can use a very limited number of grammatical structures and simple sentence patterns that he/she has learnt by repeated use (e.g. *My name is ...*).	Can use simple grammatical structures that have been learnt and practised in class. Makes frequent basic mistakes with tenses, prepositions, and personal pronouns, though when he/she is speaking or writing about a familiar topic the meaning is generally clear.	Can communicate with reasonable accuracy on familiar topics (those being studied or occurring frequently during the school day). Meaning is clear despite errors. Unfamiliar situations or topics present a challenge, however, particularly when the connection to familiar patterns is not obvious.
Phonological control	Can pronounce a very limited repertoire of learnt and familiar words and phrases. Native speakers who are aware of what the pupil has been learning and familiar with the pronunciation patterns of pupils from different language backgrounds can understand his/her pronunciation, but sometimes with difficulty.	Can pronounce familiar words (those being learnt in class or used in the school generally) in a reasonably clear manner, though with a noticeable foreign accent. It is sometimes necessary to ask the pupil to repeat what he/she has said.	Can pronounce words with confidence in a clearly intelligible way. Some mispronunciations still occur, but in general he/she is closely familiar with the sounds of English.
Orthographic control (if appropriate to the age of the pupil)	Can copy keywords from the board, flashcards or posters. Can copy or write his/her name, address and the name of the school.	Can copy or write short sentences or phrases related to what is being studied in class. Sentence breaks are generally accurate. Words that he/she uses orally may be written with phonetic accuracy but inaccurate spelling.	Can produce short pieces of continuous writing that are generally intelligible throughout. Spelling, punctuation and layout are accurate enough to be followed most of the time.

David Little and Barbara Lazenby Simpson

Food and clothes

Appendix 5 Revised units of work (2003)

		A1 Breakthrough	A2 Waystage	B1 Threshold
Understanding	**Listening**	Can recognize and understand the words for key items of clothing (coat, shoes, etc.).	Can understand instructions given about clothing for a particular purpose (e.g. going on a school trip).	Can understand classroom talk, including stories, containing a wide range of vocabulary related to food/clothing.
		Can recognize and understand the words for the key items of a school uniform.	Can understand rules about bringing particular foods to school (e.g., chewing gum, crisps, etc.) and the reason for the rules.	
		Can recognize and understand the words for key items of food typically brought to school by pupils (e.g. sandwich, apple, biscuit).		
		Can understand routine classroom instructions about food or clothing (e.g. *Put on your apron for painting*).		
	Reading (if appropriate to the age of the pupil)	Can recognize and understand the names of basic foods.	Can read and understand the menu from a café or fast-food outlet.	Can read and understand about healthy eating, using the food pyramid for illustration.
		Can recognize and understand the names of the principal items of clothing	Can read and understand the names of foods typically seen in the supermarket.	
			Can read and understand simple descriptions of food or clothing that occur in a story.	

Food and clothes—continued

		A1 Breakthrough	A2 Waystage	B1 Threshold
Speaking	Spoken interaction	Can request basic items of food/drink in a shop. Can ask how much an item costs. Can respond non-verbally (e.g. with a nod or shake of the head) or with single-word or very brief answers to questions about the food/drink and clothes he/she likes or dislikes.	Can ask and answer basic questions about the food/drink he/she likes or dislikes and briefly report the likes and dislikes of others. Can discuss a menu and select what he/she would like. Can answer questions about items and types of clothing, e.g. what is suitable for different kinds of weather.	Can repeat an instruction given by the teacher regarding food or clothing. Can engage in discussion about clothing/fashion and food/drink, expressing personal preferences.
	Spoken production	Can use key words and simple phrases/ sentences to describe likes and dislikes (e.g. I do not like green apples, I like my new coat).	Can use a series of phrases and sentences to describe the type of meal that he/she likes best. Can use a series of phrases and sentences to describe the events surrounding a meal of particular importance in the family (e.g. a religious festival, New Year, etc.).	Can describe his/her favourite items of clothing and explain why he/she likes them. Can explain the importance of particular foods in his/her family or culture. Can explain the importance of particular items of clothing in his/her family or culture.
Writing	Writing (if appropriate to the age of the pupil)	Can copy or write lists of different foods (fruits, vegetables, meats, etc.) Can copy or write lists of clothing according to contexts of use (e.g. outdoor, indoor, school, sports).	Can write a short text describing an event in which food plays a central role (e.g. a family celebration). Can write short texts describing his/her favourite items of clothing.	Can write in an age-appropriate way about clothes/fashion and food/drink. Can write instructions for making a dish/meal that he/she likes.

David Little and Barbara Lazenby Simpson

Weather

		A1 Breakthrough	A2 Waystage	B1 Threshold
Understanding	**Listening**	Can recognize and understand basic words related to weather (e.g. *sun, rain, snow, hot, cold*) when they are spoken or read aloud.	Can follow at a general level weather-related topics covered in the mainstream class provided key vocabulary and concepts have been studied in advance and there is appropriate visual support.	Can watch a weather forecast on television and understand the main points. Can understand the key vocabulary used by the teacher to explain a unit in the textbook relating to weather.
	Reading (if appropriate to the age of the pupil)	Can recognize and understand basic words related to weather when they appear on a weather chart or flash cards or in a simple text.	Can use the pictures in a textbook to identify and understand key information about weather (*rain, wind, temperature,* etc.). Can identify and understand words to do with weather in stories and other texts.	Can identify and understand the key words in, e.g. a geography text relating to weather and can use them to categorize further information in the text (e.g. the effects of wind).
Speaking	**Spoken Interaction**	Can respond non-verbally (e.g. with a nod or shake of the head) or with single-word or very brief answers to basic questions about the weather (e.g. *Is it cold outside?*) and the kind of weather he/she likes and dislikes.	Can respond to questions about the weather he/she likes. Can take part in discussion about the weather in Ireland and about the clothing necessary for different types of weather.	Can ask and answer questions about types of weather and the effects of weather on lifestyle.
	Spoken Production	Can use simple phrases and sentences to make a short, possibly incomplete, statement about the weather.	Can use a series of phrases and sentences, with appropriate adjectives, to describe in simple terms the weather outside the classroom.	Can compare the weather in Ireland with weather in other parts of the world.

	A1 Breakthrough	A2 Waystage	B1 Threshold
Writing (if appropriate to the age of the pupil)	Can copy or write basic words to do with the weather. Can copy from the board short sentences about the weather (e.g., when writing 'news').	Can write sentences about the clothes that are necessary for different types of weather. Can write a short text about 'a perfect day'.	Can write a short letter describing the weather in Ireland and the types of clothing and other items that are necessary for different kinds of weather. Can write a short text describing the influence of weather on people in different parts of the world.

David Little and Barbara Lazenby Simpson

Using the CEF to develop English courses for teenagers at the British Council Milan

Andrew Manasseh

Overview

This chapter draws on work carried out at the British Council teaching centre in Milan. It explains the background which led to the incorporation of elements of the Common European Framework into the design and delivery of courses at the centre. Examples are given of the way in which 'can do' statements have been adapted to provide learning aims for specific groups, and of the components of a revised portfolio which has been produced. The results of an initial evaluation are given.

Introduction

The Council of Europe level system has been adopted by many institutions and is widely understood by parents and children in Italy.

In reviewing our work at the British Council teaching centre in Milan, we identified a number of advantages in adopting aspects of the broader Common European Framework:

- We wanted to provide our students of all ages with a guide to learning at the British Council. The European Language Portfolio contains useful features which we were able to adapt to suit our own audiences.
- Since one of our aims is to describe our students' progress in terms of competences, rather than just content, skills, or knowledge, we adapted the Council of Europe's 'can do' statements. We called the re-worked statements 'Student Learning Aims'. They are easy to understand and linked to class work. Our aim is to help our students recognize what they can do with the language.
- We were able to link these learning aims to classroom work by producing teachers' versions which show the connection between the 'can do' statement and the unit and section in the course book and supplementary resources.
- Learning aims also provided a focus for continual monitoring of learner progress.

In this chapter I will describe the courses that we deliver to teenagers, both at Scuola Media Inferiore level (equivalent of junior high school, ages 11–14) and Scuola Superiore level, which is the 14–18 age group. I will describe the new features of courses that we introduced, drawing on the CEF, and explain how we have attempted to evaluate these changes.

The British Council Teaching Centre, Milan

In the Milan Teaching Centre we teach children between the ages of 4 and 18, and adults at all levels from beginner to proficiency level. Our aim is to promote wider and more effective learning of the English language in Milan.

Courses at the British Council

Most students register for a one-year course which begins in October and finishes in mid-June. These courses consist of 90 academic hours taught over 30 weeks, which means that they attend two 90-minute sessions per week. Normally, students study for one academic year to reach the next British Council level (see Figure 1).

Most of the teenage students attend British Council lessons from 15.00–16.30, after state school which generally finishes a 13.30 or 14.00.

We also have once-a-week lessons for Scuola Media Inferiore level (ages 11–14) who, for reasons of other school commitments, are unable to attend twice a week.

Why do parents decide to send their children to the British Council?

All teenage students in Italy receive some English language lessons at school, although the range and extent of the input depends upon the type of school. The 'progetto lingue 2000' has been highly successful in encouraging schools and parents to get students to level A2 at the end of Scuola Media Inferiore (aged 14) and level B1 at the end of Scuola Superiore (aged 18). The B1 level is recognized for credits towards degree courses at many Italian universities.

Council of Europe levels
A system within a recognized framework

The British Council used to have an 8-level system going from level 1 (Beginners) to level 8 (Proficiency). These levels did not correlate directly to the ALTE (Association of Language Testers in Europe) or Council of Europe levels, and we regularly received enquiries from parents about their children's levels compared to the British Council courses. We therefore decided to show the equivalences between British Council courses and the Council of Europe levels. These are set out in Figure 1.

New BC Level	COE Level	Cambridge exam	Age ranges	School ages
Beginner	A1	Starters	6–8	Scuola Elementare
Elementary	A1	Movers, Flyers	6–10	Scuola Elementare
Pre Intermediate	A2	KET	10–16	Scuola Inferiore Scuola Superiore
Intermediate 1	B1		10–16	Scuola Inferiore Scuola Superiore
Intermediate 2	B1	PET	11–16	Scuola Inferiore Scuola Superiore
Pre Advanced	B2	First Certificate	14–18	Scuola Superiore
Advanced 1	C1		14–18	Scuola Superiore
Advanced CAE	C1	Cambridge Advanced	14–18	Scuola Superiore
Very Advanced	C2		14–18	Scuola Superiore
Very Advanced 2	C2	Proficiency	14–18	Scuola Superiore

FIGURE 1 British Council courses for children and Council of Europe levels.

Andrew Manasseh

The Portfolio—a guide for students and parents

We produced a guide to learning at our centre for teenagers, young children, and adults, based on the European Language Portfolio but adapted to our courses in Milan.

We wanted a learning guide for students and parents that informed them not only about the language courses but also about the other related services that the British Council provides. These include a Student Resource Centre which contains a wide range of English learning resources that can be borrowed, a computer section, videos, DVDs, cassettes, books and magazines, the British Council language learning website, and a multimedia study centre.

Our starting point was The Language Passport from the European Languages Portfolio (accredited model No. 06.2000). This is intended for students aged 16+ but as we wanted a guide that could be used for age groups of 11–18 we decided to retain some sections and drop others.

Adapting the European Languages Portfolio

Section 1. *Profile of Language skills—dropped*
All of our new students complete a pre-course level placement test and our existing students from previous years graduate to classes on the basis of their progress. Our assessment of their language level is sufficient to place learners in the most appropriate class.

Section 2. *Self-assessment grid—retained*
We retained this (in English and Italian) as a reference for students and parents.

Section 3. *Summary of language learning and intercultural experiences— dropped*
This section is a useful and reflective exercise for older, adult learners and less relevant to younger children.

Sections 3 and 4. *Certificates and diplomas and Equals courses attended— dropped*
This section is relevant to older learners.

The British Council portfolio

The British Council portfolio is called the Student Learning Guide and it contains the following:

1 Language learning—exercises to help you decide what you want to do in English.

These are three questionnaire style activities that are used as class discussions or for homework at the beginning of the course. (See the Appendix to this chapter.)
   1 When do you use English?
   2 What can you expect to do in class?
   3 How do you like to be assessed?

2 What you can expect from classes—methodology statement which informs students of our general teaching approach.

Our aim in all our classes is to help you use English more effectively. We help you learn **grammar and vocabulary**, as these are the building blocks of language. However, this alone won't help you to communicate. We aim to give you as many opportunities as possible to use the language to help you speak more fluently.

Some students say that they want all their **mistakes** corrected and others say that they don't want any correction, they just want to speak. The most helpful thing that your teacher can do is to correct the important mistakes and help you understand how to improve.

As well as speaking we also work on your reading, writing and listening skills. Good communication relies on being able to **understand** what is being said to you, therefore we help you to develop your ability to understand everyday speech. Reading and writing are also good ways of revising language and extending the range of your vocabulary.

For almost all our courses the syllabus and Learning Aims are linked to a **course book**. Your teachers will use this a lot, but to make the course more interesting for you your teacher will include other materials and exercises. Don't worry if you don't use all of the book—your teacher will cover all the syllabus and the Learning Aims.

We use a **variety** of teaching techniques—such as role-plays, quizzes, discussion and games. We hope these make your lessons more enjoyable, but these activities also have a language learning point. Our teachers will explain why they are doing an activity in class: we want you to understand why we teach you in a certain way.

FIGURE 2 British Council Milan methodology statement.

3 *Language levels—where are you now?*
Self assessment grid from the Passport of the European Language Portfolio (accredited model No. 06.2000).

4 *Tools for the job—resources that we provide to help you.*
A checklist of resources that we provide for students including course learning aims, and extra resources in the Student Resource Centre.

5 *How to measure your progress.*
A checklist of tools we use to measure progress—assessed tasks (usually homework), learning aims checks used in class, end-of-course progress tests.

6 *Learner training—ideas to help you improve your learning.*
A list of ideas to help students with their learning strategies for listening, reading, speaking, writing, and pronunciation.

7 *Homework record.*
A grid to help students record their homework and enable teachers to write comments, and grades that can be used in student and parent counselling (see Figure 3).

We think it is a good idea to keep a record (and copies) of homework that you do during the course.
Pensiamo sia utile tenere un diario dei compiti svolti durante il corso, ed i lavori stessi.

Andrew Manasseh

Date	Description	Comments/grade

FIGURE 3 Homework record sheet.

Student learning aims

We examined the competency-based 'can do' statements (see Document 2 in the Reference documents section of this book) and saw a central role for using these as part of our courses. We adapted them so that the wording is more accessible to younger learners and so that, more importantly, teachers, students, and parents can perceive a clear link between the course book and the 'can do' statements. They allow us to help students to realize why they are studying, what they can actually do with the language, and how they are progressing.

We use published ELT course books with all of our standard courses for children. We formed project teams of teachers who cross-referenced the Council of Europe 'can do' statements to relevant sections in the course books.

This gives teachers an easy reference between the course book activities/tasks and the competency.

What learning aims are

We provided different definitions of learning aids to meet the needs of different users.

Definition given to academic and customer service staff

Learning Aims are signposts for students to enable them to understand why they are learning certain language points/topics.

Learning Aims should help students (and teachers) to informally assess their competences—and indicate what they need to be able to do next. We use end-of-course tests and external exams for more formal testing.

Learning Aims are there to help us explain to students our choice of syllabus. This does not prevent students from requesting topics/areas that interest them.

Teachers help students link these to the classroom activities and tasks. We have prepared teachers' versions which refer each aim to the corresponding section in the course book.

Explanation of learning aims for students and parents
The Student Learning Guide (portfolio) contains the following explanatory notes for students and their parents.

Your teacher will give you a set of Learning Aims for your course. These Learning Aims are linked to 'Can do' statements that are included in the Common European Framework.

For example: 'I can ask for ask for things in a polite way, using the correct grammar and show that I can understand the answer.'

To be able to do this you will study the language of question words, the word order, use of modal auxiliary verbs (can, may, could) and practise this language in situations—such as in a classroom or a shop.

Example of learning aims

An example of learning aims for intermediate 1 class teenagers (14–18 years old) based on CEF Level B1 is given in Figure 4.

	☺	☺	☹
Speaking			
I can start, maintain and close simple face to face conversation on topics that are familiar or of personal interest.			
I can maintain a conversation or discussion on a range of familiar subjects.			
I can give and seek personal views or opinions.			
I can deal with most situations that arise when making travel arrangements or when travelling.			
I can agree and disagree politely.			
I can express and respond to feelings such as surprise, happiness, sadness, interest.			
Listening			
I can generally follow extended discussion if the speech is quite slow and clear.			
I can follow clear speech in everyday conversation but sometimes I need words/phrases to be repeated.			
I can understand the main points of a radio or TV programme and simpler recorded materials on topics of personal interest that are slow and clear.			
Reading			
I can understand the main points in short newspaper articles about topics that are familiar.			
I can read columns or interviews in newspapers and magazines where an opinion is given on a topic and understand the overall meaning of the text.			
I can skim (read quickly) short texts and find relevant facts and information, e.g. who, what, where, when.			
I can understand the plot of a clearly structured story and recognize what the most important episodes and events are and what is significant about them.			
Writing			
I can fill in a form.			
I can write simple connected texts on a range of topics that I am interested in and can give personal views and opinions.			
I can write simple texts about experiences or event, for example, about a trip, for a school newspaper or a club newsletter.			
I can write an informal letter to a friend, giving news (narrating an event, describing a trip, talking about future plans).			

FIGURE 4 Example of learning aims for intermediate 1 class teenagers (14–18 years old) based on CEF level B1.

Andrew Manasseh

We produced teachers' versions of the learning aims which show the link between the 'can do' statement and the unit, section, or exercise in the course book and extra resources that we have available.

The teachers' version was designed to help teachers to cross-reference the course book exercises with the competence, so that they can develop lessons which reflect learning aims. We also identified extra resources that they can use.

An example is shown in Figure 5.

	Speaking / listening	Textbook Reference	Supplementary resources*
S/L 1	I can ask and respond to questions about what people do at work and in their free time (what do you do … ?)	Unit 1 p 6–7	P: RP—31a 'The things you should know about dreams' Revision pres simple G: Grammar—2 tense review.doc G: Grammar—2 Revision sheet G: Grammar—2 Basic question formation
S/L 2	I can make and respond to common social expressions (how are you doing? Pleased to meet you …)	Unit 1 p 13	
S/L 3	I can understand language used to talk about basic personal information, shopping, and school.	Unit 2 p 16–17	P: CGE—'2 Chit Chat' Pres simp P: RP—1 Who are you? Pres simp qs P: RP—5 But what are they doing? Pres cont G: Grammar—2 Asking questions G: Grammar—2 Pres simp & Pres cont G: Grammar—2 Pres simp questions
S/L 4	I can talk about things that I have or own and want to have (I have got … have you got … ?)	Unit 2 p 14–16 Unit 2 p 17	P: CGE—'11 Home sweet home' Pres simp qs P: CGE—'24 Flatmates' Habits P: RP—2 Talk about routines P: RP—3 Spot the similarities House vocab G: Reading—Guess the furniture G: Reading—Household chores G: Grammar—Adverbs of frequency

FIGURE 5 Teachers' version of the learning aims.

Note. The supplementary resources include paper based resource packs for teachers. The copyright allows these to be photocopied for classroom use. Example P: RP—31a 'The things you should know about dreams' Revision pres simple. This comes from Reward Pre-Intermediate (Susan Kay, Heinemann 1994). The materials with titles G: (example G: Grammar—2 tense review.doc) are written by British Council teachers and are copyright British Council.

How do we use learning aims in class?

The learning aims are not designed as a formal assessment mechanism as we have end-of-course tests and encourage students to take external exams, such as those from Cambridge ESOL, Trinity College London, and other examination boards in order to obtain certification. The learning aims are seen as an integral part of the learning process rather than an assessed outcome.

We set up regular learning aims reviews that take place as class activities.

| Instructions to students | The Student Learning Guide (portfolio) contains the following instructions. |

Your teacher will remind you of the Learning Aims during the course. You should be able to tick off (✓) things from the list that you can do or can do better in English.

| Instructions to teachers | This is given to teachers. |

We need to justify to our students what we are teaching them. We need to explain to them why we teach them in a certain way and guide them as to how they can learn most effectively.

The course book syllabus shows **what** they are learning, the Learning Aims indicate **why** and the Student Learning Guide (portfolio) has some advice on **how**.

Beginner to Intermediate (A1–B2)
Ask students to read through the Learning Aims (A1 and A2 levels are available in Italian and English).

Two questions to ask
1 Do they remember exercises/activities that they have done in class that help them with these 'Can do' statements?
2 Do they feel more confident doing these things in English?

If they feel more confident then they can tick them off. Remember the review is informal and designed to show the link between the courses and the Council of Europe 'Can do' statements.

Advanced levels (C1 and C2)
At higher levels it is more appropriate to get students to reflect on what they have been studying in order show the link to the Council of Europe 'Can do' statements in the European Language Portfolio.

Read through the Learning Aims with the students.
1 Do they remember exercises/activities that they have done in class that help them with these 'Can do' statements?
2 Do they feel more confident doing these things in English?
3 Are there skills/language points that they would like further practice in?

They can do this at home for homework or in class and put notes in the 'Comments section'. You can use a copy of the European Language Portfolio if this helps demonstrate the link between the course and the Council of Europe.

Evaluation

In March 2003, we wanted to find out which course features students found essential, important, nice but not important, or neither important nor useful. So, we conducted a questionnaire survey. The results are given in Figure 6.

Andrew Manasseh

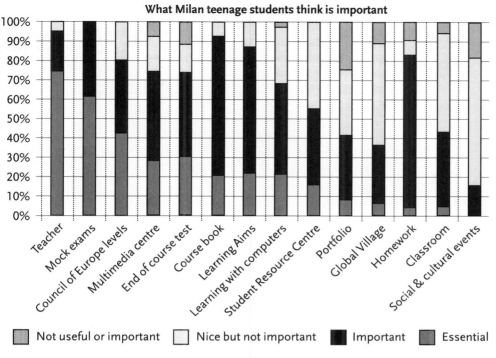

FIGURE 6 Survey results.

Obviously the students value their teacher very highly, as we would hope. A lot of our students seem to value the Learning Aims and the link to the Council of Europe levels. However, these results need to be treated with caution; we haven't probed the answers yet. This initial survey does give us some interesting pointers about the features we must get right and the others which we need to develop further or communicate better so that their added value is perceived.

We intend to gather feedback and evaluate satisfaction and attitudes to these features from students, parents, and teaching staff.

Focus group research with current students

We are planning to conduct further research with focus group interviews:
- Fully structured—where the interviewer follows a specific question order and completes a structured questionnaire.
- Semi-structured—the interviewers follow a questionnaire but obtain further detail with more open ended questions.
- Unstructured—the interviewer has a topic guide to follow, and guides a discussion.

Possible questionnaire

A possible questionnaire for use in this survey is reproduced in Figure 7.

These elements of my course are valuable	I agree strongly	I agree slightly	I disagree slightly	I disagree strongly
The link to Council of Europe levels				
The Language Learning Portfolio				
The start of course activities 1 When do you use English? 2 What can you expect in class? 3 How do you like to be assessed?				
How we measure your progress 1 End of course test 2 Mid-course assessment 3 Homework				
The learning aims				
The learning aims check activities				
Homework				
The study facilities at the British Council 1 The Multimedia Centre 2 The Student Resources Centre				

FIGURE 7 A possible survey questionnaire.

Conclusion

We are still learning how we can best use the Council of Europe levels, the learning aims, and the Portfolio to inform the process of change we have begun.

We believe that what we do is now done better and communicated better. We and the students understand what we want to achieve, and we are all being challenged to deliver it.

We have questions about how to go forward from here, such as how we are going to develop the learning aims so that they are more readily adaptable to other course books or courses with no books We also want to investigate ways of incorporating learner training into the learning process.

References

European Language Portfolio, accredited model No. 06.2000. 2000 Lang Edizioni: Milano.

Progetto Lingua Lombardia European Language Portfolio accredited model No. 30.2002. 2002 M.I.U.R. Ufficio Scolastico Regione per la Lombardia.

The author

Andrew Manasseh is currently the Deputy Director of the British Council in Milan. From 1998–2001 he managed and taught on a variety EFL programmes/teacher training projects for the British Council in Prague. He managed the business programme and wrote a range of Business English skills course materials for the British Council Bangkok from 1995–8. He has also taught EFL to teenagers and adults in Japan, France, and Italy.

Appendix   Activities to help students to decide what they want to do in English.

We trialled a number of activities and opted for the ones that received the most positive feedback from teachers and students.

We have included three reflective classroom activities which are designed to sensitize students to their learning needs and priorities. We envisage the teacher focusing on these activities in the first two classes as a way of setting the scene for the course. We also want to encourage students to gather and keep evidence of their learning.

1 When do you use English?   Here are some ideas—think about when you use English and which things you would like to do better. Add some of your own ideas and discuss these with your teacher and your class mates.

When do you use English?	Often	Sometimes	Never	I would like to do this more often
I meet and talk to people who speak English.				
I write e-mails/letters/postcards in English.				
I watch TV , DVDs, and videos in English.				
I watch films at the cinema in English.				
I use the Internet and look at English websites.				
I have to study some subjects in English at school.				
I speak English on holidays.				
I chat with friends on the Internet in English.				

2 What can you expect to do in class?   These are some of the types of activity you'll be doing in class. Tick them off as you do them and then decide how enjoyable you found them

Activity	Done	Enjoyable	Not enjoyable
a speaking to my classmates in pairs or groups in English			
b doing roleplays and drama activities in pairs or groups			
c listening to songs in English			
d watching video clips in English			
e reading articles from books, magazines and newspapers			
f writing letters, articles or short stories			
g playing language games			
h studying grammar rules			
i doing project work, e.g. making a class magazine or researching a topic of interest			
j using CD-Roms or the Internet			

3 How do you like to be assessed?

Assessment
To find out how my English is progressing, I would like ...

Activities	Done	Useful	Not useful	Comments
a the teacher to correct all my oral mistakes in class				
b my classmates to correct my oral mistakes				
c to have regular written tests in class				
d the teacher to correct my homework				
e to correct my homework myself				
f to talk to the teacher about my work				
g				
h				

Andrew Manasseh

Using the CEF to develop English courses for adults at the University of Gloucestershire

Piers Wall

Overview

This chapter looks at the work currently being carried out at Cheltenham International Language Centre (CILC), the English language centre at the University of Gloucestershire. It describes the background leading to the incorporation of the 'can do' elements of the Common European Framework into the design and delivery of courses at the centre. It also describes the process by which this change was implemented, and the implications it has had for other aspects of the curriculum.

Background

The centre delivers a number of English language courses including General English, and preparation for IELTS and Cambridge ESOL examinations. These courses are taught to multilingual classes and are mostly full-time (15 hours a week) running over terms of approximately 12 weeks throughout the year. All the courses have a syllabus for each specific skill area (reading, writing, listening, and speaking) and for language areas such as grammar, vocabulary, and functions. The courses use a course book. Assessment is based on written progress tests, writing tasks, and tutor perceptions during the course.

Levels

The centre has started to use the Council of Europe levels to show the relationship between the General English courses, and external examinations.

CILC Level	Council of Europe level	Cambridge Examination
Elementary	A1	
Pre-intermediate	A2	KET
Intermediate	B1	PET
Upper Intermediate	B2	FCE
Lower Advanced	C1	CAE

Issues

A number of factors came together which led us to question whether the way in which courses were programmed was indeed the best approach. These were as follows:

1 The increasing number of long-term students

There was an increase in the numbers of long-term students with specific reasons for learning English, e.g. for work, or for future study at an English speaking college or university. Such students had specific aims and goals which the courses needed to meet.

2 The increasing number of students from China

The increasing number of students from China, from a totally different academic culture, was having an impact on courses and multilingual classes. These students found it difficult to adjust to courses which developed 'general' skills and language use, rather than preparing them directly and explicitly for their assessments. This was particularly true of low-level students who needed to develop their overall language level, skills, and use but whose focus tended to be on achieving the IELTS score they needed. These students were able to understand and respond to given targets, however.

3 Attitudes to General English

Given the increasing number of students with specific aims and goals, there was some indication that students were not convinced that a General English course would meet their requirements. Students were not able to see the value in developing language and skills to help them achieve their goals. Coursebooks did not necessarily provide the reassurance that they were looking for, and weekly programmes were not explicit enough to show how the programme would help them with their goals. This was particularly true of low-level students who intended to study at college or university, who felt they should be studying for IELTS whatever their level.

4 Over reliance on coursebooks when programming

The system for developing course programmes put the coursebook at the centre of the course. The template for course plans referred to the number of units covered within a week, and the teaching guidelines encouraged tutors to divide the number of coursebook units up into the number of weeks in the term and to add supplementary materials as necessary.

5 Tutor observation

As a part of the formal tutor observation programme, tutors had been asked to complete a cover sheet for their observed lesson. This asked them not only to identify the learner outcomes for the particular lesson, but also to identify how the particular lesson related to the overall aims and outcomes of the course and the curriculum. Tutors had found this latter section difficult to complete and had requested further guidance on this area.

6 Learner training skills

There was a need to build specific study and learner training skills into the programme on a regular basis. Although activities such as how to use an English/English dictionary and how to record vocabulary were promoted in the first two weeks of the course, it was important that these

Piers Wall

skills were recycled and developed as the course progressed. This would also help students see their relevance.

7 Examinations
There was a need to promote more explicitly lower-level examinations such as Cambridge ESOL Key English Test (KET) and Preliminary English Test (PET), and to show students the value of these in helping them to achieve their long term goals.

Taken together, these issues suggested that there was a need to develop something which would enable:

- students to identify clearly the aims and outcomes of the course on which they were studying
- students to see the relevance of skills and language development in helping them achieve their goals
- students and tutors to see how individual lessons related to the overall aims and outcomes of the course
- students and tutors to determine whether they had achieved the outcomes in all areas via identifiable assessments which related to the course aims and outcomes
- tutors to plan towards the aims and outcomes of the course rather than the course book.

The Council of Europe framework and 'can do' statements

I had been directed to the published version of the Common European Framework (Council of Europe 2001) at several sessions at the IATEFL Conference in York (April 2002). The book included examples of 'can do' statements at the various Council of Europe levels. (See Document 1 in the Reference documents section of this book.)

The advantage of using the 'can do' statements were:

- We already referred to these levels in our course descriptions.
- Cambridge examinations were also defined in terms of these levels so they would be familiar to tutors and students. This would also guide us with any additions or amendments to the CEF 'can do' statements.
- The 'can do' statements would indicate to students what they were expected to do by the end of the course/level.
- The statements would provide a substantial basis on which tutors could programme a course.
- The statements would help tutors to relate individual lessons to the course outcomes.

There were some obstacles to overcome, particularly the number of different areas included in the CEF and the complexity of the language used in the 'can do' examples.

Developing 'can do' statements

The chart shown in Figure 1 was presented to a group of teaching staff in December 2002 as the basis for a discussion in the curriculum development sessions.

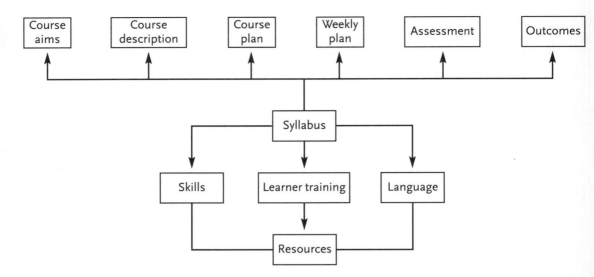

FIGURE 1 Elements of course design.

Sample 'can do' statements from the Council of Europe framework were also presented. It was agreed that the curriculum development sessions would be used to try and develop 'can do' statements for the General English courses from level A1 to C1. The following points were also agreed:

- To ensure parity with the CEF versions, Cambridge ESOL examinations would be used as a guideline.
- Statements would be developed only for the areas which tutors were familiar with, i.e. grammar, vocabulary, function, reading, listening, speaking, and writing.
- Reference to non-Cambridge ESOL tasks, e.g. talking about a topic would also be included at what was deemed an appropriate level.
- There would be statements for pronunciation and study skills.

Tutors were paired up to work on specific levels and asked to produce draft 'can do' statements for each area.

By the end of the week, we had developed draft statements for the five General English levels. They related to the Cambridge ESOL examinations at different levels, but also included some IELTS type tasks at B2 levels and above.

The process had raised a number of issues, particularly the impact the statements would have on programming, progress tutorials, and assessments. There was also the issue of writing them in language accessible to the students.

The initial implications of the developments were that:

- courses would be based on the 'can do' statements rather than the coursebook. This would require a significant change for some tutors.
- weekly programmes would need to refer to the statements both in terms of the outcomes for individual lessons and, more significantly, for the week as a whole.

- progress tutorial forms would need to refer explicitly to the 'can do' statements, and students would need to be given a clear indication of their performance in working towards these.
- for some areas, e.g. speaking, explicit assessment tasks and criteria would need to be developed, rather than using the current continuous assessment approach.
- students would need to be aware of the 'can do' statements and how lessons and weekly programmes related to these.
- study skills would need to be a regular feature of the programme, as opposed to being introduced only at the beginning of the course, as had tended to happen previously.

Introducing the statements

At the beginning of 2003, the remaining teaching staff were introduced to the 'can do' statements and to the implications outlined above. Although some staff were sceptical as to how this might work, it was agreed to try the statements and review at the end of the spring term. Speaking tasks and criteria were developed (from the Cambridge ESOL examinations), and tutorial forms were amended to refer to the 'can do' statements. Students were all given a copy of the statements for their level.

Evaluation

The first evaluation took place at the end of the spring term. Issues that had arisen included:
- the difficulty of introducing the statements to students who had studied the previous term
- the need to simplify the language (not just at the lower levels)
- the need to increase the number of progress tutorials to help direct students to their progress via the statements
- the need to number the statements
- the need to include the statement numbers in the weekly programme
- the need to review the use of particular course books.

In spite of these issues, there were some positive responses the 'can do' introduction:
- Teaching staff indicated in evaluations that the principle of the 'can do' statements was a good one, and that it might enable students to reflect on their ability and progress more effectively.
- Some tutors felt they made programming easier. Subsequent evaluations have supported this.
- Student evaluations indicated the statements are perceived as helpful, although there is still an issue of making the statements understandable at the lower levels. The current set of 'can do' statements given to students at level B1 is set out in the Appendix to this chapter.
- Weekly programmes have become more focused on the aims and the outcomes of the course, and the use of supplementary materials has increased significantly.
- The sample of the weekly programme (Figure 2) shows the current practice of highlighting the learner outcomes and relating these to the 'can do' statements.

University of Gloucestershire
Cheltenham International Language Centre
General English Weekly Plan

Class DEE	Level C1	Tutors Judith and Jane	Course book	Landmark Adv.	Term 1	Week 3

Outcomes.

By the end of this week students will have …

- practised fluency and accuracy in speaking, using a range of tenses and worked on self-correction (Can do 2/4/9/22/25)
- worked on note-taking skills, listening for detail and gist (Can do 11/12/13/48)
- developed their vocabulary of time and space, crime and punishment (Can do 45/46/56/57)
- practised writing summaries from notes and describing past events using a range of tenses (Can do 26/31/33/60/61)
- extended their reading skills, looking at different text types and how a text is linked (Can do 36/41/42).

Day	Monday	Tuesday	Wednesday	Thursday	Friday
Tutors	Judith and Jane	Judith and Jane	Judith and Jane	Judith and Jane	Judith
Lesson Focus Topic	Function Wishing	Listening Time Travel	Writing Summaries of facts	Speaking/Vocabulary Crime and punishment	Function (Obs) Talking about the past Life changes
Materials	C/b p.21 Skls.Pls Grm/Spk u.25	C/b p. 22	Writing Tasks 7.3 C/b p. 22	C/b p. 26	Skl.Pls.Grm/Spk u14
Lesson Focus Topic	Reading skills Fact and fiction Rain/Science	Function (Obs) Speculating and Hypothetical situations	Reading/vocabulary Civilisation and Language	Listening Recounting bad Experiences	Video/listening skills Space
Materials	C/b p. 20/21 www.scienceshack	C/b p. 23 Pairwork3 u.15 Conv.Gamb.44	C/b p. 24	C/b p. 28/29	Authentic TV.
Homework	W/b p. 14 Time travel notes	W/b p. 15	Write a summary	Vocab. notes W/b p. 19	Diaries — a famous criminal. W/b p. 19

Student comments

FIGURE 2 Sample weekly programme.

- Lesson observations have also indicated tutors have become far more aware of the relationship between the individual lesson and its relationship with the course aims and curriculum.
- Students are starting to be more aware of their strengths, and of areas to work on.
- Tutor feedback on course books is more focused and analytical.

The future

Having introduced the 'can do' statements into the syllabus, we now need to continue to develop and review their use. As part of our future developments, we plan to:

- review current statements with a view to continuing to simplify the language used and to ensuring they are in line with the CEF versions
- introduce statements for areas such as interaction
- relate assessments and progress tutorials explicitly to 'can do' statements
- introduce 'can do' benchmark statements into initial placement testing
- continue to explore the relationship between the 'can do' statements, the syllabus, the progress tutorials and the assessments
- cross reference coursebooks and supplementary materials to 'can do' statements at each level to make programming easier, and to encourage further use of supplementary materials
- evaluate coursebooks on their 'can do' potential, and use the evaluation to influence future coursebook choices
- encourage more explicit feedback from students through evaluations.

References

Council of Europe. 2001. *Common European Framework of Reference for Languages: Learning, teaching, assessment.* Cambridge: Cambridge University Press.
Also available for download from http://www.coe.int/T/E/Cultural_Co-operation/education/Languages/Language_Policy/Common_Framework_of_Reference/1cadre.asp#TopOfPage

The author

Piers Wall is currently the Head of Cheltenham International Language Centre (CILC), the English language centre at the University of Gloucestershire. He has overall responsibility for the academic management of the EFL and teacher training programmes. He is also a trainer and assessor for the Cambridge CELTA. In addition to teaching and training in the UK, he has also taught EFL to young learners, teenagers, and adults in Portugal and Spain.

Appendix

'Can do' statements given to students at level B1.

Speaking

1 I can communicate with native speakers in familiar situations and participate in a conversation.

2 I can participate in discussions on familiar everyday topics.

3 I can briefly give reasons and explanations for opinions and plans.

4 I can give simple descriptions of places, experiences, and situations.

5 I can tell a simple story and talk about a book or film and describe how I felt about it.

6 I can recognize when I need to make my language formal and I can do this.

7 I can respond to spontaneous conversations on topics with which I am familiar.

8 I can correct some of my errors when I speak and those of other students.

Listening

I can listen to short recordings about familiar topics that contain mostly language with which I am familiar and that are relatively clear.

9 I can predict the content of these recordings, based on pictures and written information.

10 I can listen and get a general understanding of these recordings.

11 I can understand the main points of these recordings.

12 I can understand most details of these recordings.

13 I can follow a conversation, providing the topic is familiar.

14 I can understand the main point of some television programmes on familiar topics when the delivery is clear.

15 I can understand some of the dialogue in films if the accent is familiar.

16 I can understand information in a context with which I am familiar.

17 I can understand some information on the telephone if the situation is familiar.

18 I can begin to understand relationships between speakers.

19 I can recognize levels of formality in familiar social situations.

Reading

I can read short texts about familiar topics that contain mostly language with which I am familiar

20 I can predict the content of these texts before reading, based on pictures, headlines, and layout.

21 I can read these texts and gain a general understanding.

22 I can understand the main ideas of these texts and details of these texts.

23 I can understand the details of these texts.

24 I can begin to understand writers' opinions and feelings.

25 I can begin to understand the structure of language when it is used to link ideas of time, place, and possession.

Piers Wall

26 I can identify and understand a range of text types from public notices and signs to letters.

27 I can read and understand short stories at the appropriate level.

Writing

28 I can write simple, logical, and connected texts (100–50 words) on topics which are familiar, or of personal interest, e.g. family, holidays, everyday routine.

29 I can write a range of text types including letters, narratives, and descriptions of people, objects, and places.

30 I can complete forms and questionnaires at the appropriate level and communicate information.

31 I can write personal texts, which include descriptions of experiences and feelings, e.g. an embarrassing event, the happiest day of my life, a film I enjoyed.

32 I can connect my ideas logically using a limited range of expressions, e.g. linking words and time expressions.

33 I can spell known words accurately.

34 I can punctuate and paragraph appropriately.

35 I can begin to correct my own work and that of others.

36 I can keep a diary which records my problems and progress and in which I practise writing on given topics.

Study skills

37 I can use an English to English dictionary at the appropriate level and select the appropriate use of a word or phrase.

38 I can use a dictionary to find out the pronunciation, grammar, and meaning of a word.

39 I can keep useful and appropriate records of new vocabulary and phrases for reference and self-study, e.g. wordlists. I can update and use these regularly.

40 I can keep useful and appropriate records of coursework in an accessible file or folder.

41 I can make useful notes on the main points from reading and listening sources at the appropriate level and from the whiteboard.

42 I can use my notes to complete tables, short written texts, and short talks.

43 I can organize my own studies in my free time and meet deadlines.

44 I can realistically assess my own performance and that of the other students at my level.

45 I can edit and correct my own work.

46 I can take responsibility for my own progress and work independently on my weaker areas and I know when I need help from others.

Pronunciation

47 I can be understood when I speak, most of the time, although I make some pronunciation errors.

48 I can show an awareness of syllable, word, and sentence stress.

49 I can begin to produce appropriate intonation.

50 I can begin to assess my pronunciation.

51 I am aware of the phonemic chart and I can produce the individual sounds.

52 I am aware of my own pronunciation problems.

Vocabulary

53 I can use a range of vocabulary to talk about a variety of everyday topics and issues, e.g. holidays, families, work.

54 I can select appropriate vocabulary to talk about feelings, opinions, and experiences, e.g. happiness, sadness, anger.

55 I can begin to recognize there are different types of phrasal verbs and can understand and use a number of phrasal verbs and collocations.

56 I can choose vocabulary appropriate to context.

57 I can start to work out the meaning of unknown vocabulary items from context.

58 I can form other words in a word family group based on my knowledge of how nouns, adjectives, etc. are formed.

Grammar

59 I can use the grammar structures listed effectively, although I may make some mistakes.

60 I can use the English tense system to talk about the past, present, and future using the structures listed.

61 I can use some linking words and phrases to express the relationship between ideas, e.g. although, however.

62 I can try to use some of the more complex structures.

63 I can self-correct basic errors.

Piers Wall

Reference documents

Proficient user	C2	Can understand with ease virtually everything heard or read. Can summarize information from different spoken and written sources, reconstructing arguments and accounts in a coherent presentation. Can express him/herself spontaneously, very fluently and precisely, differentiating finer shades of meaning even in more complex situations.
	C1	Can understand a wide range of demanding, longer texts, and recognize implicit meaning. Can express him/herself fluently and spontaneously without much obvious searching for expressions. Can use language flexibly and effectively for social, academic and professional purposes. Can produce clear, well-structured, detailed text on complex subjects, showing controlled use of organizational patterns, connectors and cohesive devices.
Independent user	B2	Can understand the main ideas of complex text on both concrete and abstract topics, including technical discussions in his/her field of specialization. Can interact with a degree of fluency and spontaneity that makes regular interaction with native speakers quite possible without strain for either party. Can produce clear, detailed text on a wide range of subjects and explain a viewpoint on a topical issue giving the advantages and disadvantages of various options.
	B1	Can understand the main points of clear standard input on familiar matters regularly encountered in work, school, leisure, etc. Can deal with most situations likely to arise whilst travelling in an area where the language is spoken. Can produce simple connected text on topics which are familiar or of personal interest. Can describe experiences and events, dreams, hopes and ambitions and briefly give reasons and explanations for opinions and plans.
Basic user	A2	Can understand sentences and frequently used expressions related to areas of most immediate relevance (e.g. very basic personal and family information, shopping, local geography, employment). Can communicate in simple and routine tasks requiring a simple and direct exchange of information on familiar and routine matters. Can describe in simple terms aspects of his/her background, immediate environment and matters in areas of immediate need.
	A1	Can understand and use familiar everyday expressions and very basic phrases aimed at the satisfaction of needs of a concrete type. Can introduce him/herself and others and can ask and answer questions about personal details such as where he/she lives, people he/she knows and things he/she has. Can interact in a simple way provided the other person talks slowly and clearly and is prepared to help.

Reference document 1
Common reference levels:
global scale

Taken from: Council of Europe. 2001. *Common European Framework of Reference for Languages: Learning, Teaching, Assessment.* Cambridge: Cambridge University Press.

Also available for download from http://www.coe.int/T/E/Cultural_Co-operation/education/Languages/Language_Policy/Common_Framework_of_Reference/1cadre.asp#TopOfPage. © Council of Europe 2003

Level		Global descriptor (CEF Table 1)	Salient characteristics (CEF Section 3.5, simplified)
			It cannot be overemphasized that Level C2 is not intended to imply native-speaker competence or even near native-speaker competence. Both the original research and a project using CEF descriptors to rate mother-tongue as well as foreign language competence (North 2002: CEF Case Studies volume) showed the existence of ambilingual speakers well above the highest defined level (C2). Wilkins had identified a seventh level of "Ambilingual Proficiency" in his 1978 proposal for a European scale for unit-credit schemes.
C2	Proficient user	Can understand with ease virtually everything heard or read. Can summarize information from different spoken and written sources, reconstructing arguments and accounts in a coherent presentation. Can express him/herself spontaneously, very fluently and precisely, differentiating finer shades of meaning even in more complex situations.	**Level C2**, labelled '**Mastery**', is intended to characterize the degree of precision, appropriateness and ease with the language which typifies the speech of those who have been highly successful learners. Descriptors calibrated here include: *convey finer shades of meaning precisely by using, with reasonable accuracy, a wide range of modification devices; has a good command of idiomatic expressions and colloquialisms with awareness of connotative level of meaning; backtrack and restructure around a difficulty so smoothly the interlocutor is hardly aware of it.*
C1	Proficient user	Can understand a wide range of demanding, longer texts, and recognize implicit meaning. Can express him/herself fluently and spontaneously without much obvious searching for expressions. Can use language flexibly and effectively for social, academic and professional purposes. Can produce clear, well-structured, detailed text on complex subjects, showing controlled use of organizational patterns, connectors and cohesive devices.	**Level C1** was labelled **Effective Operational Proficiency**. What seems to characterize this level is good access to a broad range of language, which allows fluent, spontaneous communication, as illustrated by the following examples: *Can express him/herself fluently and spontaneously, almost effortlessly. Has a good command of a broad lexical repertoire allowing gaps to be readily overcome with circumlocutions. There is little obvious searching for expressions or avoidance strategies; only a conceptually difficult subject can hinder a natural, smooth flow of language.* The discourse skills characterizing the previous band continue to be evident at Level C1, with an emphasis on more fluency, for example: *select a suitable phrase from a fluent repertoire of discourse functions to preface his remarks in order to get the floor, or to gain time and keep it whilst thinking; produce clear, smoothly-flowing, well-structured speech, showing controlled use of organizational patterns, connectors and cohesive devices.*
B2+	Independent user		This band (B2+) represents a **strong Vantage** performance. The focus on argument, effective social discourse and on language awareness which appears at B2 continues. However, the focus on argument and social discourse can also be interpreted as a new focus on discourse skills. This new degree of discourse competence shows itself in conversational management (co-operating strategies): *give feedback on and follow up statements and inferences by other speakers and so help the development of the discussion; relate own contribution skilfully to those of other speakers.* It is also apparent in relation to coherence/cohesion: *use a variety of linking words efficiently to mark clearly the relationships between ideas; develop an argument systematically with appropriate highlighting of significant points, and relevant supporting detail.* Finally, it is at this band that there is a concentration of items of negotiating.
B2	Independent user	Can understand the main ideas of complex text on both concrete and abstract topics, including technical discussions in his/her field of specialization. Can interact with a degree of fluency and spontaneity that makes regular interaction with native speakers quite possible without strain for either party. Can produce clear, detailed text on a wide range of subjects and explain a viewpoint on a topical issue giving the advantages and disadvantages of various options	Descriptors calibrated at **Level B2** represent quite a break with the content so far. For example at the lower end of the band there is a focus on effective argument: *account for and sustain his opinions in discussions by providing relevant explanations, arguments and comments; explain a viewpoint on a topical issue giving the advantages and disadvantages of various options; develop an argument giving reasons in support of or against a particular point of view; take an active part in informal discussion in familiar contexts, commenting, putting point of view clearly, evaluating alternative proposals and making and responding to hypotheses.* Secondly, running right through the level there are two new focuses. The first is being able to more than hold your own in social discourse: e.g. *understand in detail what is said to him/her in the standard spoken language even in a noisy environment; initiate discourse, take his turn when appropriate and end conversation when he/she needs to, though he/she may not always do this elegantly; interact with a degree of fluency and spontaneity that makes regular interaction with native speakers quite possible without imposing strain on either party.* The second new focus is a new degree of language awareness: *correct mistakes if they have led to misunderstandings; make a note of "favourite mistakes" and consciously monitor speech for it/them; generally correct slips and errors if he becomes conscious of them.*

Reference document 1a
The common reference levels with salient characteristics

Taken from: Council of Europe. 2003. 'Relating Language Examinations to the Common European Framework of Reference for Languages: Learning, Teaching, Assessment (CEF). Preliminary Pilot Version of a Proposed Manual' DGIV/EDU/LANG (2003) 5, Stasbourg
© Council of Europe 2003

Level	Global descriptor (CEF Table 1)	Salient characteristics (CEF Section 3.5, simplified)
B1+		This band (B2+) seems to be a **strong Threshold** performance. The same two main features at B1 continue to be present, with the addition of a number of descriptors which focus on the exchange of quantities of information, for example: *provide concrete information required in an interview/consultation (e.g. describe symptoms to a doctor) but does so with limited precision; explain why something is a problem; summarize and give his or her opinion about a short story, article, talk, discussion interview, or documentary and answer further questions of detail; carry out a prepared interview, checking and confirming information, though he/she may occasionally have to ask for repetition if the other person's response is rapid or extended; describe how to do something, giving detailed instructions; exchange accumulated factual information on familiar routine and non-routine matters within his field with some confidence.*
B1	Can understand the main points of clear standard input on familiar matters regularly encountered in work, school, leisure, etc. Can deal with most situations likely to arise whilst travelling in an area where the language is spoken. Can produce simple connected text on topics which are familiar or of personal interest. Can describe experiences and events, dreams, hopes & ambitions and briefly give reasons and explanations for opinions and plans.	**Level B1** reflects the **Threshold Level** specification and is perhaps most categorized by two features. The first feature is the ability to main interaction and get across what you want to, in a range of contexts, for example: *generally follow the main points of extended discussion around him/her, provided speech is clearly articulated in standard dialect; express the main point he/she wants to make comprehensibly; keep going comprehensibly, even though pausing for grammatical and lexical planning and repair is very evident, especially in longer stretches of free production.* The second feature is the ability to cope flexibly with problems in everyday life, for example *cope with less routine situations on public transport; deal with most situations likely to arise when making travel arrangements through an agent or when actually travelling; enter unprepared into conversations on familiar topics.*
A2+		This band (A2+) represents a **strong Waystage** (A2+) performance. What is noticeable here is more active participation in conversation given some assistance and certain limitations, for example: *understand enough to manage simple, routine exchanges without undue effort; make him/herself understood and exchange ideas and information on familiar topics in predictable everyday situations, provided the other person helps if necessary; deal with everyday situations with predictable content, though he/she will generally have to compromise the message and search for words;* plus significantly more ability to sustain monologues, for example: *express how he feels in simple terms; give an extended description of everyday aspects of his environment e.g. people, places, a job or study experience; describe past activities and personal experiences; describe habits and routines; describe plans and arrangements; explain what he/she likes or dislikes about something.*
A2	Can understand sentences and frequently used expressions related to areas of most immediate relevance (e.g. very basic personal and family information, shopping, local geography, employment). Can communicate in simple and routine tasks requiring a simple and direct exchange of information on familiar and routine matters. Can describe in simple terms aspects of his/her background, immediate environment and matters in areas of immediate need.	**Level A2** appears to reflect the level referred to by the **Waystage** specification. It is at this level that the majority of descriptors stating social functions are to be found, like use simple everyday polite forms of greeting and address; greet people, ask how they are and react to news; handle very short social exchanges; ask and answer questions about what they do at work and in free time; make and respond to invitations; discuss what to do, where to go and make arrangements to meet; make and accept offers. Here too are to be found descriptors on getting out and about: the simplified cut-down version of the full set of transactional specifications in "The Threshold Level" for adults living abroad, like: make simple transactions in shops, post offices or banks; get simple information about travel; use public transport: buses, trains, and taxis, ask for basic information, ask and give directions, and buy tickets; ask for and provide everyday goods and services.
A1	Can understand and use familiar everyday expressions and very basic phrases aimed at the satisfaction of needs of a concrete type. Can introduce him/herself and others and can ask and answer questions about personal details such as where he/she lives, people he/she knows and things he/she has. Can interact in a simple way provided the other person talks slowly and clearly and is prepared to help.	**Level A1** is the lowest level of generative language use—the point at which the learner can interact in a simple way, ask and answer simple questions about themselves, where they live, people they know, and things they have, initiate and respond to simple statements in areas of immediate need or on very familiar topics, rather than relying purely on a very finite rehearsed, lexically organized repertoire of situation-specific phrases.

		A1	A2	B1
Understanding	**Listening**	I can recognize familar words and very basic phrases concerning myself, my family and immediate concrete surroundings when people speak slowly and clearly.	I can understand phrases and the highest frequency vocabulary related to areas of most immediate personal relevance (e.g. very basic personal and family information, shopping, local area, employment). I can catch the main point in short, clear, simple messages and announcements.	I can understand the main points of clear standard speech on familiar matters regularly encountered in work, school, leisure, etc. I can understand the main point of many radio or TV programmes on current affairs or topics of personal or professional interest when the delivery is relatively slow and clear.
	Reading	I can understand familiar names, words and very simple sentences, for example on notices and posters or in catalogues.	I can read very short, simple texts. I can find specific, predictable information in simple everyday material such as advertisements, prospectuses, menus and timetables and I can understand short simple personal letters.	I can understand texts that consist mainly of high frequency everyday or job-related language. I can understand the description of events, feelings and wishes in personal letters.
Speaking	**Spoken Interaction**	I can interact in a simple way provided the other person is prepared to repeat or rephrase things at a slower rate of speech and help me formulate what I'm trying to say. I can ask and answer simple questions in areas of immediate need or on very familiar topics.	I can communicate in simple and routine tasks requiring a simple and direct exchange of information on familiar topics and activities. I can handle very short social exchanges, even though I can't usually understand enough to keep the conversation going myself.	I can deal with most situations likely to arise whilst travelling in an area where the language is spoken. I can enter unprepared into conversation on topics that are familiar, of personal interest or pertinent to everyday life (e.g. family, hobbies, work, travel and current events).
	Spoken Production	I can use simple phrases and sentences to describe where I live and people I know.	I can use a series of phrases and sentences to describe in simple terms my family and other people, living conditions, my educational background and my present or most recent job.	I can connect phrases in a simple way in order to describe experiences and events, my dreams, hopes and ambitions. I can briefly give reasons and explanations for opinions and plans. I can narrate a story or relate the plot of a book or film and describe my reactions.
Writing	**Writing**	I can write a short, simple postcard, for example sending holiday greetings. I can fill in forms with personal details, for example entering my name, nationality and address on a hotel registration form.	I can write short, simple notes and messages relating to matters in areas of immediate need. I can write a very simple personal letter, for example thanking someone for something.	I can write simple connected text on topics which are familiar or of personal interest. I can write personal letters describing experiences and impressions.

Reference document 2
Self assessment grid

Taken from: Council of Europe. 2001. *Common European Framework of Reference for Languages: Learning, Teaching, Assessment.* Cambridge: Cambridge University Press.

Also available for download from http://www.coe.int/T/E/Cultural_Co-operation/education/Languages/Language_Policy/Common_Framework_of_Reference/1cadre.asp#TopOfPage. © Council of Europe 2003

Reference documents

B2	C1	C2
I can understand extended speech and lectures and follow even complex lines of argument provided the topic is reasonably familiar. I can understand most TV news and current affairs programmes. I can understand the majority of films in standard dialect.	I can understand extended speech even when it is not clearly structured and when relationships are only implied and not signalled explicitly. I can understand television programmes and films without too much effort.	I have no difficulty in understanding any kind of spoken language, whether live or broadcast, even when delivered at fast native speed, provided I have some time to get familiar with the accent.
I can read articles and reports concerned with contemporary problems in which the writers adopt particular attitudes or viewpoints. I can understand contemporary literary prose.	I can understand long and complex factual and literary texts, appreciating distinctions of style. I can understand specialized articles and longer technical instructions, even when they do not relate to my field.	I can read with ease virtually all forms of the written language, including abstract, structurally or linguistically complex texts such as manuals, specialized articles and literary works.
I can interact with a degree of fluency and spontaneity that makes regular interaction with native speakers quite possible. I can take an active part in discussion in familiar contexts, accounting for a sustaining my views.	I can express myself fluently and spontaneously without much obvious searching for expressions. I can use language flexibly and effectively for social and professional purposes. I can formulate ideas and opinions with precision and relate my contribution skilfully to those of other speakers.	I can take part effortlessly in any conversation or discussion and have a good familiarity with idiomatic expressions and colloquialisms. I can express myself fluently and convey finer shades of meaning precisely. If I do have a problem I can backtrack and restructure around the difficulty so smoothly that other people are hardly aware of it.
I can present clear, detailed descriptions on a wide range of subjects related to my field of interest. I can explain a viewpoint on a topical issue giving the advantages and disadvantages of various options.	I can present clear, detailed descriptions of complex subjects integrating sub-themes, developing particular points and rounding off with an appropriate conclusion.	I can present a clear, smoothly flowing description or argument in a style appropriate to the context and with an effective logical structure which helps the recipient to notice and remember significant points.
I can write clear, detailed text on a wide range of subjects related to my interests. I can write an essay or report, passing on information or giving reasons in support of or against a particular point of view. I can write letters highlighting the personal significance of events and experiences.	I can express myself in clear, well-structured text, expressing points of view at some length. I can write about complex subjects in a letter, an essay or a report, underlining what I consider to be the salient issues. I can select style appropriate to the reader in mind.	I can write clear, smoothly flowing text in an appropriate style. I can write complex letters, reports or articles which present a case with an effective logical structure which helps the recipient to notice and remember significant points. I can write summaries and reviews of professional or literary works.

Domain	Locations	Institutions	Persons
Personal	Home: house, rooms, garden own of family of friends of strangers Own space in hostel, hotel The countryside, seaside	The family Social networks	(Grand)Parents, offspring, siblings, aunts, uncles, cousins, in-laws, spouses, intimates, friends, acquaintances
Public	Public spaces: street, square, park Public transport Shops (super)markets Hospitals, surgeries, clinics Sports stadia, fields, halls Theatre, cinema, entertainment Restaurant, pub, hotel Places of worship	Public authorities Political bodies The law Public health Services clubs Societies Political parties Denominations	Members of the public Officials Shop personnel Police, army, security Drivers, conductors Passengers Players, fans, spectators Actors, audiences Waiters, barpersons Receptionists Priests, congregation
Occupational	Offices Factories Workshops Ports, railways Farms Airports Stores, shops Service industries Hotels Civil Service	Firms Multinational corporations Nationalized industries Trade unions	Employer/ees Managers Colleagues Subordinates Workmates Clients Customers Receptionists, secretaries Cleaners
Educational	Schools: hall, classrooms, playground, Sports fields, corridors Colleges Universities Lecture theatres Seminar rooms Student Union Halls of residence Laboratories Canteen	School College University Learned societies Professional Institutions Adult education bodies	Class teachers Teaching staff Caretakers Assistant staff Parents Classmates Professors, lecturers (Fellow) students Library and laboratory staff Refectory staff, cleaners Porters, secretaries

Reference document 3
External contexts of use

Taken from: Council of Europe. 2001. *Common European Framework of Reference for Languages: Learning, Teaching, Assessment*. Cambridge: Cambridge University Press.

Also available for download from http://www.coe.int/T/E/Cultural_Co-operation/education/Languages/Language_Policy/Common_Framework_of_Reference/1cadre.asp#TopOfPage. © Council of Europe 2003

Reference documents

Objects	Events	Operations	Texts
Furnishing and furniture Clothing Household equipment Toys, tools, personal hygiene Objets d'art, books Wild/domestic animals, pets Trees, plants, lawn, ponds Household goods Handbags Leisure/sports equipment	Family occasions Encounters Incidents, accidents Natural phenomena Parties, visits Walking, cycling, motoring Holidays, excursions Sports events	Living routines: dressing, undressing, cooking, eating, washing, DIY, gardening Reading, radio, and TV Entertaining Hobbies Games and sports	Teletext Guarantees Recipes Instructional material Novels, magazines Newspapers Junk mail Brochures Personal letters Broadcast and recorded spoken texts
Money, purse, wallet Forms Goods Weapons Rucksacks Cases, grips Balls Programmes Meals, drinks, snacks Passports, licences	Incidents Accidents, illnesses Public meetings Law-suits, court trials Rag-days, fines, arrests Matches, contests Performances Weddings, funerals	Buying and obtaining public services Using medical services Journeys by road/rails/ ship/air Public entertainment and leisure activities Religious services	Public announcements and notices Labels and packaging Leaflets, graffiti Tickets, timetables Notices, regulations Programmes Contracts Menus Sacred texts, sermons, hymns
Business machinery Industrial machinery Industrial and craft tools	Meetings Interviews Receptions Conferences Trade fairs Consultations Seasonal sales Industrial accidents Industrial disputes	Business admin. Industrial management Production operations Office procedures Trucking Sales operations Selling, marketing Computer operation Office maintenance	Business letter Report memorandum Life and safety notices Instructional manuals Regulations Advertising material Labelling and packaging Job description Sign posting Visiting cards
Writing material School uniforms Games equipment and clothing Food Audio-visual equipment Blackboard and chalk Computers Briefcases and school bags	Return to school/entry Breaking up Visit and exchanges Parents' days/evenings Sports days, matches Disciplinary problems	Assembly Lessons Games Playtime Clubs and societies Lectures, essay writing Laboratory work Library work Seminars and tutorials Homework Debates and discussions	Authentic texts (as above) Textbooks, readers Reference books Blackboard text OP text Computer screen text Videotext Exercise materials Journal articles Abstracts Dictionaries

	Range	Accuracy	Fluency	Interaction	Coherence
C2	Shows great flexibility reformulating ideas in differing linguistic forms to convey finer shades of meaning precisely, to give emphasis, to differentiate and to eliminate ambiguity. Also has a good command of idiomatic expressions and colloquialisms.	Maintains consistent grammatical control of complex language, even while attention is otherwise engaged (e.g. in forward planning, in monitoring others' reactions).	Can express him/herself spontaneously at length with a natural colloquial flow, avoiding or backtracking around any difficulty so smoothly that the interlocutor is hardly aware of it.	Can interact with ease and skill, picking up and using non-verbal and intonational cues apparently effortlessly. Can interweave his/her contribution into the joint discourse with fully natural turntaking, referencing, allusion making, etc.	Can create coherent and cohesive discourse making full and appropriate use of a variety of organizational patterns and a wide range of connectors and other cohesive devices.
C1	Has a good command of a broad range of language allowing him/her to select a formulation to express him/herself clearly in an appropriate style on a wide range of general, academic, professional or leisure topics without having to restrict what he/she wants to say.	Consistently maintains a high degree of grammatical accuracy; errors are rare, difficult to spot and generally corrected when they do occur.	Can express him/herself fluently and spontaneously, almost effortlessly. Only a conceptually difficult subject can hinder a natural, smooth flow of language.	Can select a suitable phrase from a readily available range of discourse functions to preface his remarks in order to get or to keep the floor and to relate his/her own contributions skilfully to those of other speakers.	Can produce clear, smoothly flowing, well-structured speech, showing controlled use of organizational patterns, connectors and cohesive devices.
B2+					
B2	Has a sufficient range of language to be able to give clear descriptions, express viewpoints on most general topics, without much conspicuous searching for words, using some complex sentence forms to do so.	Shows a relatively high degree of grammatical control. Does not make errors which cause misunderstanding, and can correct most of his/her mistakes.	Can produce stretches of language with a fairly even tempo; although he/she can be hesitant as he/she searches for patterns and expressions. There are few noticeably long pauses.	Can initiate discourse, take his/her turn when appropriate and end conversation when he/she needs to, though he/she may not always do this elegantly. Can help the discussion along on familiar ground confirming comprehension, inviting others in, etc.	Can use a limited number of cohesive devices to link his/her utterances into clear, coherent discourse, though there may be some 'jumpiness' in a long contribution.

Reference document 4
Qualitative aspects of spoken language use

Taken from: Council of Europe. 2001. *Common European Framework of Reference for Languages: Learning, Teaching, Assessment*. Cambridge: Cambridge University Press.

Also available for download from http://www.coe.int/T/E/Cultural_Co-operation/education/Languages/Language_Policy/Common_Framework_of_Reference/1cadre.asp#TopOfPage. © Council of Europe 2003

Reference documents

	RANGE	ACCURACY	FLUENCY	INTERACTION	COHERENCE
B1+					
B1	Has enough language to get by, with sufficient vocabulary to express him/herself with some hesitation and circumlocutions on topics such as family, hobbies and interests, work, travel, and current events.	Uses reasonably accurately a repertoire of frequently used 'routines' and patterns associated with more predictable situations.	Can keep going comprehensibly, even though pausing for grammatical and lexical planning and repair is very evident, especially in longer stretches of free production.	Can initiate, maintain and close simple face-to-face conversation on topics that are familiar or of personal interest. Can repeat back part of what someone has said to confirm mutual understanding.	Can link a series of shorter, discrete simple elements into a connected, linear sequence of points.
A2+					
A2	Uses basic sentence patterns with memorized phrases, groups of a few words and formulae in order to communicate limited information in simple everyday situations.	Uses some simple structures correctly, but still systematically makes basic mistakes.	Can make him/herself understood in very short utterances, even though pauses, false starts and reformulation are very evident.	Can answer questions and respond to simple statements. Can indicate when he/she is following but is rarely able to understand enough to keep conversation going of his/her own accord.	Can link groups of words with simple connectors like 'and', 'but' and 'because'.
A1	Has a very basic repertoire of words and simple phrases related to personal details and particular concrete situations.	Shows only limited control of a few simple grammatical structures and sentence patterns in a memorized repertoire.	Can manage very short, isolated, mainly pre-packaged utterances, with much pausing to search for expressions, to articulate less familiar words, and to repair communication.	Can ask and answer questions about personal details. Can interact in a simple way but communication is totally dependent on repetition, rephrasing and repair.	Can link words or groups of words with very basic linear connectors like 'and' or 'then'.

Reception

Interaction

Production

Reference document 5
List of sub-scales contained in the CEF

Integrated reception and production
- Note-taking (Lectures, Seminars etc.) (English: page 96)
- Processing Text (English: page 96)

Aspects of communicative language competence
Linguistic
- General Linguistic Range (English: page 110)
- Vocabulary Range (English: page 112)
- Vocabulary Control (English: page 112)
- Grammatical Accuracy (English: page 114)
- Phonological Control (English: page 117)
- Phonological Control (English: page 118)

Socio-linguistic
- Socio-linguistic Appropriateness (English: page 122)

Pragmatic
- Flexibility (English: page 124)
- Turntaking (repeated) (English: page 124)
- Thematic Development (English: page 125)
- Coherence and Cohesion (English: page 125)
- Spoken Fluency (English: page 129)
- Propositional Precision (English: page 129)

	Overall	Range	Coherence	Accuracy	Description	Argument
C2	Can write clear, *highly accurate and smoothly flowing complex texts in an appropriate and effective personal style conveying finer shades of meaning*. Can use a logical structure which helps the reader to find significant points.	Shows great flexibility in *formulating ideas in differing linguistic forms to convey finer shades of meaning precisely, to give emphasis and to eliminate ambiguity*. Also has a good command of idiomatic expressions and colloquialisms.	Can create coherent and cohesive texts making full and appropriate use of a variety of organizational patterns and a wide range of connectors and other cohesive devices.	Maintains consistent *and highly accurate grammatical control of even the most complex language forms. Errors are rare and concern rarely used forms.*	Can write clear, smoothly flowing and fully engrossing stories and descriptions of experience in a style appropriate to the genre adopted.	Can produce clear, smoothly flowing, complex reports, articles and essays which present a case or give critical appreciation of proposals or literary works. Can provide an appropriate and effective logical structure which helps the reader to find significant points.
C1	Can write clear, well-structured *and mostly accurate texts of* complex subjects. Can underline the relevant salient issues, *expand and support* points of view at some length with subsidiary points, reasons and relevant examples, and round off with an appropriate conclusion.	Has a good command of a broad range of language allowing him/her to select a formulation to express him/herself clearly in an appropriate style on a wide range of general, academic, professional or leisure topics without having to restrict what he/she wants to say. *The flexibility in style and tone is somewhat limited.*	Can produce clear, smoothly flowing, well-structured text, showing controlled use of organizational patterns, connectors and cohesive devices.	Consistently maintains a high degree of grammatical accuracy; *occasional errors in grammar, collocations and idioms.*	Can write clear, detailed, well-structured and developed descriptions and imaginative texts in an assured, personal, natural style appropriate to the reader in mind.	Can write clear, well-structured expositions of complex subjects, underlining the relevant salient issues. Can expand and support point of view with subsidiary points, reasons and relevant examples.
B2	Can write clear, detailed *official and semi-official texts on a variety* of subjects related to his field of interest, synthesizing and evaluating information and arguments from a number of sources. *Can make a distinction between formal and informal language with occasional less appropriate expressions.*	Has a sufficient range of language to be able to give clear descriptions, express viewpoints on most general topics, using some complex sentence forms to do so. *Language lacks, however, expressiveness and idiomaticity and use of more complex forms is still stereotypic.*	Can use a limited number of cohesive devices to link his/her sentences into clear, coherent text, though there may be some "jumpiness" in a longer text.	Shows a relatively high degree of grammatical control. Does not make errors which cause misunderstandings.	Can write clear, detailed descriptions of real or imaginary events and experiences marking the relationship between ideas in clear connected text, and following established conventions of the genre concerned. Can write clear, detailed descriptions on a variety of subjects related to his/her field of interest. Can write a review of a film, book or play.	Can write an essay or report that develops an argument systematically with appropriate highlighting of significant points and relevant supporting detail. Can evaluate different ideas or solutions to a problem. Can write an essay or report which develops an argument, giving reasons in support of or against a particular point of view and explaining the advantages and disadvantages of various options. Can synthesize information and arguments from a number of sources.

Reference document 6
Written assessment criteria

Taken from: Council of Europe. 2003. 'Relating language examinations to the Common European Framework of reference for languages: Learning, teaching, assessment (CEF). Preliminary Pilot Version of a Proposed Manual' DGIV/EDU/LANG (2003) 5, Strasbourg. © Council of Europe 2003

Reference documents

Level						
	of interest, by linking a series of shorter discrete elements into a linear sequence. The texts are understandable but occasional unclear expressions and/or inconsistencies may cause a break-up in reading.	him/herself with some circumlocutions on topics such as family, hobbies and interests, work, travel, and current events.	connected, linear text.	*"routines" and patterns associated with more common situations. Occasionally makes errors that the reader usually can interpret correctly on the basis of the context.*	simple connected text. Can write a description of an event, a recent trip—real or imagined. Can narrate a story. Can write straightforward, detailed descriptions on a range of familiar subjects within his field of interest.	give his/her opinion about accumulated factual information on a familiar routine and non-routine matters, within his field with some confidence. Can write very brief reports to a standard conventionalized format, which pass on routine factual information and state reasons for actions.
A2	Can write a series of simple phrases and sentences linked with simple connectors like "and", "but" and "because". *Longer texts may contain expressions and/or show coherence problems which makes the text hard to understand.*	Uses basic sentence patterns with memorized phrases, groups of a few words and formulae in order to communicate limited information in simple everyday situations.	Can link groups of words with simple connectors like "and", "but" and "because".	Uses simple structures correctly, but still systematically makes basic mistakes. *Errors may sometimes cause misunderstandings.*	Can write short simple imaginary biographies and simple poems about people. Can write very short, basic descriptions of events, past activities and personal experiences.	
A1	Can write simple isolated phrases and sentences. *Longer texts contain expressions and show coherence problems which makes the text very hard or impossible to understand.*	Has a very basic repertoire of words and simple phrases related to personal details and particular concrete situations.	Can link words or groups of words with very basic linear connectors like "and" and "then".	Shows only limited control of a few simple grammatical structures and sentence patterns in a memorized repertoire.	Can write simple phrases and sentences about themselves and imaginary people, where they live and what they do.